D0441761

CENTRAL
AMSTERDAM

Het IJ

Ijhaven

Stedelijk
Museum CS

THE EAST

Oude
Kerk
Museum
Amstelkring

ENTRUM

Oosterdok

Oosterdok

CHINATOWN

Rosse
Buurt

Museum Het
Rembrandthuis

Nederlands
Scheepvaart
Museum

JODENHOEK

Amstel

Museum
Willet
Holthuysen

Natura
Artis
Magistra

Joods
Historisch
Museum

Magere
Brug

Tropenmuseum

Oosterpark

OOST

DE PIJP

Sarphatipark

CITYPACK TOP 25
Amsterdam

TERESA FISHER
ADDITIONAL WRITING BY HILARY WESTON AND JACKIE STADDON

If you have any comments
or suggestions for this guide
you can contact the editor at
Citypack@theAA.com

AA Publishing
Find out more about AA Publishing and the wide
range of services the AA provides by visiting our
website at www.theAA.com/travel

How to Use This Book

KEY TO SYMBOLS

🚩 Map reference to the accompanying fold–out map

✉ Address

☎ Telephone number

🕐 Opening/closing times

🍴 Restaurant or café

🚆 Nearest rail station

Ⓜ Nearest subway (Metro) station

🚌 Nearest bus/tram route

⛴ Nearest riverboat or ferry stop

♿ Facilities for visitors with disabilities

❓ Other practical information

▷ Further information

ℹ Tourist information

✋ Admission charges:
Expensive (over €5),
Moderate (€3–5), and
Inexpensive (€3 or less)

★ Major Sight   ★ Minor Sight

👣 Walks   🚍 Excursions

🏬 Shops

🎭 Entertainment and Nightlife

🍴 Restaurants

This guide is divided into four sections
• Essential Amsterdam: an introduction to the city and tips on making the most of your stay.
• Amsterdam by Area: we've broken the city into five areas, and recommended the best sights, shops, entertainment venues, nightlife and restaurants in each one. Suggested walks help you to explore on foot.
• Where to Stay: the best hotels, whether you're looking for luxury, budget or something in between.
• Need to Know: the info you need to make your trip run smoothly, including getting about by public transport, weather tips, emergency phone numbers and useful websites.

Navigation In the Amsterdam by Area chapter, we've given each area its own colour, which is also used on the locator maps throughout the book and the map on the inside front cover.

Maps The fold–out map accompanying this book is a comprehensive street plan of Amsterdam. The grid on this fold–out map is the same as the grid on the locator maps within the book. We've given grid references within the book for each sight and listing.

Contents

Introducing Amsterdam

How do you define Amsterdam? To some it's canals, carillons ringing out from church steeples and the variety of the Dutch gable. To others it's synonymous with tolerance—of eccentricity and of experimentation, of red light districts and smoking cafés.

Amsterdam is tiny—you can cross it on foot in 30 minutes—just 740,000 people packed into not quite enough space. Yet it rewards frequent visits, and it has a changing schedule of special exhibitions, festivals and arts events—from the wackiest avant-garde shows to the works of Rembrandt or Vermeer. The many faces of Amsterdam help make it among Europe's most popular short-break destinations.

Amsterdam feels like a big village. Amsterdammers' sociability makes it easy to get to know people—as does the fact that many speak several languages. Intellectual, curious about the world and great talkers, it is not surprising that Amsterdammers have dared to embark on some of the great social experiments of our time. It sometimes seems that where Amsterdam, with the rest of the Netherlands, leads, the world generally follows—though maybe a few centuries later. Prostitution has been tolerated in Amsterdam since the 17th century. Amsterdam's liberal drug laws allow licensed cafés to permit the sale of cannabis. Amsterdam invented traffic calming—tough laws and schemes to discourage cars and improve driving conditions—and it may yet become the first city to ban cars outright. Laws permit euthanasia and gay marriages. Informality is the norm—local business people long ago abandoned suits and ties, and most restaurants are unpretentious. Many a street corner has a *bruine kroeg* (brown café), named after the mellow hue of the tobacco-stained walls where people comfortably settle down with a newspaper or argue over the issues of the day with friends and regulars.

Facts + Figures

- Bicycles—600,000
- Houseboats—2,500
- Windmills—6
- Canals—165
- Bridges—1,281
- Statues and sculptures—302
- Flower bulbs in parks—600,000

A BOLD IDEA

Radical politicians of the 1970s came up with the bold idea of providing free bicycles, painted white, which everyone could use. Although it seemed a good idealistic incentive, the idea floundered when the bikes were stolen, repainted and sold. Now the white bikes are back—but this time they can only be unlocked using an electronic smart card.

QUEEN'S DAY

Nothing better sums up Amsterdam than *Koninginnedag* (Queen's Day), the unstuffy monarch's official birthday (30 April) and the occasion for a wild city-wide street party. Even radical Amsterdammers celebrate. Everyone wears orange, the royal shade, and the gay community dons tiaras, tinsel and fancy dress. More than a million people take part.

CYCLE CITY

First-time visitors may well be mown down by a speeding bicycle within a few moments of arrival. Designated cycle paths through the city often run contrary to the traffic flow, so look both ways before crossing any road. Join in the fun on a bicycle without brakes—instead you have to back pedal. Never leave your bicycle unlocked.

A Short Stay in Amsterdam

DAY 1

Morning To avoid the crowds try to get to **Anne Frankhuis** (▷ 24–25) for when it opens at 9am. The experience can leave quite an impression on visitors; afterwards a quiet stroll along the canal may be the order of the day. Make your way south down to the area of the **Jordaan** (▷ 29) known as the 'nine streets', which straddle the canals from Singel to Prinsengracht. This district is full of interesting idiosyncratic shops.

Mid-morning Take a break in Huidenstraat at **Pompadour** (▷ 36), a chocolatier and tiny teashop. After wandering around here for while, make your way up to the pedestrianized Dam Square, the ceremonial and political heart of the city, dominated by the **Royal Palace** (▷ 45). The square is always crowded and full of street entertainers.

Lunch On the northern side of Dam is the city's biggest department store, **De Bijenkorf** (▷ 55). You can get a tasty meal at the store's buffet-style restaurant, **La Ruche** (▷ 64), which offers a wide variety at a good price.

Afternoon After lunch board a canal boat from the nearby jetty on Damrak, near Central Station. For about an hour you can cruise around the canal ring, take photographs and listen to a commentary in several languages.

Early evening Most people are curious to see the **Red Light District** (▷ 49) and a visit just before dinner is probably the best time to do this if you have any reservations about going. Keep to the main drag, avoiding the dark side alleys, and you will feel quite at ease.

Dinner For a chic French meal try the **Café Roux** (▷ 62) in the Grand Hotel on Oudezijds Voorburgwal or for a less expensive Indonesian option go to **Sukasari** (▷ 64) on Damstraat.

Morning Start early at the **Rijksmuseum** (▷ 85), and although much is closed for renovation it is still possible to view Rembrandt's famous *Nightwatch*. For modern art go on to the nearby **Van Gogh Museum** (▷ 86–87) to view the works of the master, but expect crowds, especially gathered around the *Sunflowers*. For those with an interest in drink rather than art make a detour to visit the **Heinken Experience** (▷ 90) in Stadhouderskade.

Mid-morning Take a break for coffee in the Van Gogh Museum before completing your tour of the masterpieces. Carry on down to the **Vondelpark** (▷ 88–89) for a breath of fresh air and a stroll in the park.

Lunch Take lunch in the park where there are several eating choices. If the weather is fine, an outdoor table is a great place for people-watching.

Afternoon The park is the favourite green space of Amsterdammers and a popular place for joggers and walkers. With its 48ha (118 acres), it makes a welcome change from the hectic city life. Leave the park by the north end to walk to the smartest shopping street in the city, P. C. Hooftstraat. Here you will find international designer names as well as local Dutch designers. After some window shopping or serious spending return to your hotel to freshen up.

Dinner Have an early evening meal at **Bodega Keyzer** (▷ 94) where musicians and concertgoers have been dining since 1903.

Evening Go next door to the magnificent **Concertgebouw** (▷ 92) for an evening of classical music or throw caution to the wind with a flutter at the Holland Casino.

Top 25

►►►

Amsterdams Historisch Museum ▷ 40–41 The place to familiarize yourself with the history of the city.

Anne Frankhuis ▷ 24–25 The most visited attraction in Amsterdam must surely be the saddest.

Begijnhof ▷ 42 A haven of spiritual tranquillity and unhurried peace in the heart of the city.

Westerkerk ▷ 28 Climb to the top of the tower for some great views across the city.

Vondelpark ▷ 88–89 This park throbs with life on a warm summer's day– great for people-watching.

Van Gogh Museum ▷ 86–87 You'll have to arrive early to see the *Sunflowers*.

Tropenmuseum ▷ 98 Vivid, vibrant story of daily life in the tropics in this extraordinary museum.

Stedelijk Museum CS ▷ 74 A must for aficionados of modern art in its temporary home.

Singel ▷ 50 Take a boat trip along the canal for the very best view of the city and learn about its history.

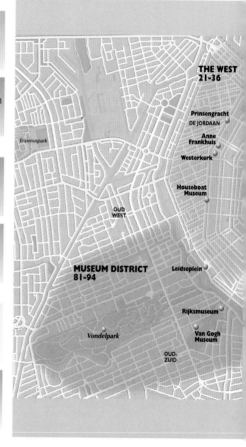

Rosse Buurt ▷ 49 In your face and brazen, most people just can't resist a look.

Rijksmuseum ▷ 85 The showcase of the artist Rembrandt and wonderful 17th-century Dutch art.

Prinsengracht ▷ 27 Checkout the stylish houseboats, often full of flowers, on this canal.

These pages are a quick guide to the Top 25, which are described in more detail later. Here they are listed alphabetically and the tinted background shows the area they are in.

Bloemenmarkt ▷ 43
Every hue and fragrance in abundance at the the city's floating market.

Herengracht ▷ 44 The grandeur of this waterway has given rise to the name the 'Gentleman's Canal'.

Houseboat Museum ▼▼▼
▷ 26 It's not every day you get to visit a houseboat museum, just as if someone is living in it.

Joods Historisch Museum
▷ 68 This museum charts the history of the city's Jewish community.

Koninklijk Paleis ▷ 45
Amsterdam's grandest secular building reveals the city's earlier wealth.

Leidseplein ▷ 84
When night falls this square is one of the liveliest places in town.

Magere Brug ▷ 69
The 'Skinny Bridge' is the most photographed bridge in Amsterdam.

Museum Amstelkring
▷ 46 Visit this tiny museum for its secret chapel in the attic.

Museum Het Rembrandthuis ▷ 70
Imagine the great artist at work here 1639–1658.

Museum Willet-Holthuysen ▷ 71
Luxury period home to view.

Nederlands Scheepvaart Museum ▷ 72–73
The highlight is the East Indiaman the *Amsterdam*.
◀ ◀ ◀

CENTRAL AMSTERDAM 37–64
Herengracht
Singel
Nieuwe Kerk
CENTRUM
Koninklijk Paleis
Amsterdams Historisch Museum
Begijnhof
Bloemenmarkt
Museum Willet Holthuysen

Museum Amstelkring
Oude Kerk
CHINATOWN
Rosse Buurt

Het IJ

Stedelijk Museum CS
IJhaven

THE EAST 65–80
Oosterdok

Nederlands Scheepvaart Museum
Museum Het Rembrandthuis
JODENHOEK
Joods Historisch Museum
Magere Brug
Amstel

Natura Artis Magistra

Tropenmuseum

Oosterpark
OOST

DE PIJP
Sarphatipark

Oude Kerk ▷ 48
A venerable building at the heart of the city's infamous Red Light District.

Nieuwe Kerk ▷ 47
Try to hear the fine 17th-century organ at Holland's coronation church.

Shopping

Amsterdam is full of fascinating quirky shops specializing in everything from toothbrushes to aboriginal art, children's comics to art-deco lamps, potted plants to exotic cut flowers, jazz CDs to cheese, beer or African masks.

Off the Beaten Track

These characterful shops are not always in the obvious places. Amsterdam's main shopping streets—Nieuwendijk and Kalverstraat—are dominated by global brands. Instead look where rents are lower: along Haarlemmerstraat, Damstraat and in the cross streets of the Canal Circle and the Jordaan. These cross streets were deliberately zoned for commercial use in the 17th century, when the canal circle was planned and thrived on the trade in furs and hides. Just go and wander down Reestraat, Hartenstraat, Berenstraat, Runstraat and Huidenstraat among the medley of small specialist shops, cafés and art galleries, which have replaced the original furriers.

Individualists

The entrepreneurs who run these shops have a passion for their product and they want to share their enthusiasm, so customers are not treated merely as consumers, but as fellow connoisseurs. Some will happily spend all day talking about their sources. Others are busy making the products they sell—gorgeously decorated hats, Venetian-style masks, recycled vintage clothing, evening dresses or costume jewellery.

CLUMPING CLOGS

Think Amsterdam and you'll probably think of clogs—or *klompen* as they are known in Dutch, a splendidly onomatopoeic word that imitates the heavy clumping sound the wooden shoes make as they stroll the city's pavements. They are carved from a single block of poplar wood and are extremely comfortable. Most, however, are sold as decorative souvenirs rather than as footwear. You'll find these painted with windmills, tulips or cheeses.

Clogs and tulips from Amsterdam are good gifts to bring home but don't forget the diamonds

Shopping with a Difference

The range of specialties and what they say about human ingenuity is incredible. For lovers of chocolate try Pompadour (▷ 36). Feeling guilty consuming all that sugar? De Witte Tandenwinkel (▷ 33) sells every imaginable colour of toothbrush and every possible flavour of toothpaste. Olivaria (✉ Hazenstraat 2A ☎ 6383552) is devoted to olive oils and De Jongejans (✉ Noorderkerk-straat 18) to eyewear—everything from vintage frames and mirrored shades to glam-rock extravaganzas. Joe's Vliegerwinkel (✉ Nieuwe Hoogstraat 19 ☎ 6250139) sells only toys that fly—bright kites, boomerangs and Frisbees. Lovers of children's and adults' comics, new and second-hand, should visit Lambiek (▷ 33). Clogs are synonmous with the Netherlands, for a selection check out De Klompenboer (▷ 78).

Blooming Wonderful

You will find more flowers and bulbs in Amsterdam than in any other European city—not just in the floating flower market, but all around the Canal Circle. What better souvenir of your stay than a bouquet of blooms—always buy blooms that are still closed—or a packet of bulbs, but be sure to check the import regulations first.

Museum shops are a good source of souvenirs from the city. Cheese and plants are popular, too

---

FLEA MARKETS

The dark days of World War II engendered a habit of thrift in the citizens of Amsterdam, and even in today's prosperous times, no true Amsterdammer ever throws anything away. Instead, everything—from dead light bulbs to ancient newspapers—gets recycled at one of the city's many flea markets. The biggest and best known is the one that surrounds two sides of the Stadhuis (Town Hall) on Waterlooplein. Stalls here mix the new, the old and the unimaginably decrepit. Pick up very serviceable second-hand clothes, craft items and jewellery, and wonder why anyone would want to buy a broken radio, chipped vase or a doll without a head. Other flea markets include De Looierand, the market at Noordermarkt.

Shopping by Theme

Whether you're looking for a department store, a quirky boutique, or something in between, you'll find it all in Amsterdam. On this page shops are listed by theme. For a more detailed write-up, see the individual listings in Amsterdam by Area.

Amsterdam by Night

Amsterdam is one of Europe's most vibrant nightlife capitals. On a mild summer's evening nothing beats just walking by the canal, or gliding along the canals in a glass-topped boat, to see the historic bridges and buildings spotlighted in white lights.

Something to Watch
There is plenty going on at the cinemas, both mainstream and art house. Don't miss the Tuschinski Theater (▷ 60) in a splendid art deco-style building.

Your Kind of Music
There is always something going on in the classical music world—many churches host choral concerts and organ recitals, the Melkweg and Paradiso nightclubs (▷ 93) have rock and pop, Maloe Melo (▷ 105) has blues and rock, the new Muziekgebouw aan 't IJ (▷ 105) has the former Muziekcentrum De IJsbreker experimental music venue and, in an adjacent hall, the Bimhius (▷ 104) has jazz.

Out on the Town
The city's nightclubs offer all kinds of entertainment, including plenty that is explicitly erotic in the Red Light District with its sex shows and somewhat sleazy bars. Rembrandtplein throngs with preparty drinkers; they head for Escape (▷ 78), Rain (▷ 79) or the more sophisiticated Schiller (▷ 79). Leidesplein is another popular spot, with its lively street cafés and bars.

CITY OF JAZZ

This is a city that adores jazz and blues, and there are scores of venues to chose from, including the legendary Bimhuis (which moved in 2005 to the new Muziekgebouw aan 't IJ) and Maloe Melo. The city hosts the International Blues Festival in mid-March (www.meervaart. nl), although it cedes to The Hague (Den Haag) the honour of hosting the renowned North Sea Jazz Festival in mid-July (www. northseajazz.nl). Both attract huge international stars.

Take a stroll in the city at night—the illuminations brighten up the canals, bridges and buildings

Eating Out

Choice is the key when eating out in
Amsterdam. Gone are the days of establish-
ments just serving rather solid Dutch food.
Take a look around and there is a great
selection of 'fusion' cooking, a miscellany of
tastes and a good range of prices.

Global Cuisine
Centuries of colonialism and a multicultural
population is reflected in the city's cuisine. The
most common of the ethnic cuisines are
Indonesian and Chinese. Dutch colonists added
their own dishes to the basic Indonesian meal
and most popular is the *rijsttafel*, which literally
means 'rice table'. With the rice the centrepiece
there can be anything from 15 to 30 dishes to
accompany it. For more traditional Dutch food
there are still small intimate restaurants serving
the authentic cuisine (▷ below). There is however, a trend towards less heavy fare, a 'New
Dutch' cooking, becoming increasingly popular.

Keeping the Price Down
If you are on a budget try the snack *eetcafés*
with good Dutch traditional food or more contemporary strylish dishes. Go for the *dagschotel*
(dish of the day) or *dagmenu* (menu of the
day). There's a good choice for vegetarians.

Practical Tips
Always reserve in advance for that special treat;
restaurants tend to be small and fill up quickly.
The Dutch like to eat early, 6.30–8, so restaurants get more full at this time. Eating out is a
laid-back, casual affair; dress code only applies
to the smartest of luxury and hotel restaurants.

AUTHENTIC DUTCH CUISINE
The most delicious dishes include *erwtensoep* (thick split-
pea soup), *stamppot* (meaty stews), *gerookte paling*
(smoked eel), *haring* (raw herring), *pannekoeken* (sweet
and tasty pancakes), *stroopwafels* (waffles) and cheeses.
The classic main course is *hutspot* (hotchpotch), another
variation of stew.

*There are plenty of unusual
venues to take a meal in
Amsterdam—on a canal or
by a windmill*

Restaurants by Cuisine

There are restaurants to suit all tastes and budgets in Amsterdam. On this page they are listed by cuisine. For a more detailed description of each restaurant, see Amsterdam by Area.

BROWN CAFÉS

Van Puffelen (▷ 36)

CAKES AND TEASHOPS

1E Klas (▷ 60)
Café Americain (▷ 94)
Café Vertigo (▷ 94)
Caffè Esprit (▷ 62)
Gelateria Jordino (▷ 35)
Greenwood's (▷ 62)
Nieuwe Kafé (▷ 63)
Pompadour (▷ 36)
La Ruche (▷ 64)
Winkel (▷ 36)

DUTCH

De Blauwe Hollander (▷ 35)
Café de Fles (▷ 80)
Dorrius (▷ 62)
De Groene Lantaarn (▷ 36)
Haesje Claes (▷ 62)
Keuken Van 1870 (▷ 62)
Moeder's Pot (▷ 36)
Piet de Leeuw (▷ 80)
De Poort (▷ 63)
Spijshuis de Dis (▷ 106)

ELEGANT DINING

De Belhamel (▷ 35)
Café Roux (▷ 62)
Christophe (▷ 35)
Le Ciel Bleu (▷ 106)
The Dylan Restaurant (▷ 35)
Le Garage (▷ 94)
De Gouden Reael (▷ 106)
Restaurant Bloesem (▷ 36)
La Rive (▷ 106)
De Roode Leeuw (▷ 63)
De Silveren Spiegel (▷ 64)
D'Vijff Vlieghen (▷ 64)

FISH

Albatros (▷ 35)
Bodega Keyzer (▷ 94)
De Oesterbar (▷ 94)
Le Pecheur (▷ 63)
Vis Aan de Schelde (▷ 106)

INDONESIAN

Aneka Rasa (▷ 60)
Bojo (▷ 35)
Indrapura (▷ 80)
Kantjil & de Tijger (▷ 62)
De Orient (▷ 94)
Sahid Jaya (▷ 64)
Sama Sebo (▷ 94)
Sarange Mas (▷ 64)
Sukasari (▷ 64)
Tempo Doeloe (▷ 80)

INTERNATIONAL

Amsterdam (▷ 106)
De Brakke Grond (▷ 60)
Café Pacifico (▷ 60)
Chez Georges (▷ 62)
Cinema Paradiso (▷ 35)
Dynasty (▷ 62)
Fromagerie Crignon Culinair (▷ 62)
De Kas (▷ 106)
Memories of India (▷ 63)
Ocho Latin Grill (▷ 63)
Pakistan (▷ 106)
Pasta e Basta (▷ 80)
Pinto (▷ 80)
El Rancho Argentinian (▷ 63)
Rose's Cantina (▷ 63)
Sea Palace (▷ 80)
Sherpa (▷ 36)
Shibli (▷ 64)
Tango (▷ 64)
Teppanyaki Nippon (▷ 64)
Toscanini (▷ 36)
Tuynhuys (▷ 64)
Le Zinc... et les Dames (▷ 80)

SNACKS AND *EETCAFÉS*

Bagels & Beans (▷ 94)
Gare de l'Est (▷ 106)
Gary's Muffins (▷ 35)
Het Karbeel (▷ 62)
Morita-ya (▷ 63)
Pancake Bakery (▷ 36)
La Place (▷ 63)
Small Talk (▷ 94)
Stads Pannekoekhuys (▷ 106)
Tapas Català (▷ 64)
Van Altena (▷ 94)

VEGETARIAN

De Bolhoed (▷ 35)
Golden Temple (▷ 80)
Hemelse Modder (▷ 80)
De Vliegende Schotel (▷ 36)

If You Like...

However you'd like to spend your time in Amsterdam, these top suggestions should help you tailor your ideal visit. Each sight or listing has a fuller write-up in Amsterdam by Area.

A DUTCH MOMENTO

Tulips from Amsterdam and many other plants from the Bloemenmarkt (▷ 43).
For clogs to wear or replica souvenirs it is worth the trip to Otten & Zoon (▷ 104).
Plates, vases and more from Heinen Handpainted Delftware (▷ 32).

SHOPS WITH CHARACTER

If you are into the retro look in your home go to Fifties Sixties (▷ 32) or Nic Nic (▷ 56).
Everything made of hemp? It's true at Hemp Works (▷ 56).
Herbs, spices and homeopathic remedies in this 1743 old-fashioned apothecary, Jacob Hooij (▷ 56).

Brightly painted clogs make great souvenirs (above). Eating outside is popular (below)

HONEST DUTCH FARE

From smoked eel to hearty stews, the cooking at Dorrius (▷ 62) is first class.
Robust home cooking can be found at De Blauwe Hollander (▷ 35). You are guaranteed huge portions.
D'Vijff Vlieghen (▷ 64) brings a more modern, lighter touch to the sometimes heavy traditional Dutch food.

BUFFETS—INDONESIAN STYLE

For your mini-buffet with a Javanese twist go to Kantjil & De Tijger (▷ 62).
For an all-vegetarian *rijsttafel* try Aneka Rasa (▷ 60) in Warmoesstraat in the heart of the Red Light District.
Plate after plate arrives in the Balinese setting of Sama Sebo (▷ 94).

Green Amsterdam—take out a bicycle, walk along the canal bank or stroll in one of the parks

A CANALSIDE VIEW

Stay at the Estheréa Hotel (▷ 110) for perfectly placed quiet spot overlooking the Singel canal (▷ 50).

More river view than canal, but the opulent De L'Europe Hotel (▷ 112) has a great position.

Located on the peaceful Keizergracht Canal, try the charming Canal House hotel (▷ 110).

THE LIVE MUSIC SCENE

Don't miss the world-famous Concertgebouw (▷ 92) for classical music par excellence.

For the very best in live jazz and blues stroll down to Alto Jazz Café (▷ 34).

From rock to reggae check out Paradiso (▷ 93), Amsterdam's best live music venue.

AMSTERDAM ON A SHOESTRING

The Stayokay hostel (▷ 109) by the Vondel Park is good value.

La Place (▷ 63) in Vroom & Dreesman department store offers an excellent value, tasty self-service meal.

If you intend to use public transport a lot, buy bulk tickets (▷ 118–119).

The world-renowned Concertgebouw was built in 1888 and designed by A. L. van Gendt

GOING OUT AND ABOUT

You can't go to Amsterdam without going on a canal cruise, by day or night (▷ 119).

Walk, jog, skate or run around the Vondelpark (▷ 88–89), the city's preferred green space.

Rent a bike (▷ 119) and join the locals for the best way to get around the city.

Wertheimpark is guarded by two sphinxes

STYLISH LIVING

Amsterdam's history is all about water and ships

If you like intimate boutique hotels with oodles of style, you will love The Dylan (▷ 112).

Classical chic at canalside Restaurant Christophe (▷ 35) serving high class French cuisine.

Take a tour around Coster Diamonds (▷ 90) and then choose your jewel.

ENTERTAINING THE KIDS

Take the Museumboat out to NEMO (▷ 76), the copper-clad hands-on science museum.

All aboard the *Amsterdam* schooner at the wonderful maritime Nederlands Scheepvaart Museum (▷ 72–73).

Be prepared to be scared at the Amsterdam Dungeon (▷ 51) with live shows, actors and a ride back in time.

QUIRKY MUSEUMS

The Tulip Museum (▷ 30) is the only museum in the world to be dedicated to Amsterdam's ubiquitous flower.

Discover all about life aboard in the quaint Houseboat Museum (▷ 26).

The unusual Tropenmuseum (▷ 98) has evocative displays from around the world.

THE BEST CANALS

The elaborate interior of the extraordinary Tropenmusem (above)

Herengracht (▷ 44)—if you take a boat trip you will go along here, but it's also great to walk beside.

Singel (▷ 50)—wider than most but there is lots of interest along its banks.

Prinsengracht (▷ 27)—check out the colourful houseboats and the merchant's houses.

Brouwersgracht (Brewers' Canal) is lined with converted warehouses, which date back to the 17th century (right)

The western area of Amsterdam is probably the most photogenic and is where the real soul of the city resides. This is very much a locals' area, with beautiful canals, lovely old houses and individual shops.

2

3

4

5

6

graacht

Nwe Wagenstr
Marnixkade
Brouwers-
Marnixstraat
Singel
gracht
Nwe. Willemsstr
Bahnhofstr
Domselaer
vinkstr

Palmgracht
Palmgracht
Palmstraat

Willems-
straat
Goudsbloem-
straat

Lindengracht
Lindengracht
Boomstraat
Lindenstraat

Marnixkade
Karthuizers-
Karthuizers-
str
str

Westerstraat
Westerstraat

**Pianola
Museum**

DE JORDAAN

Anjeliersstraat

Prinsengracht

Tuinstraat
**Tulip
Museum**
Ophoved-
kunde

Egelantiersstraat
Egelantiersgracht
Egelantiersgracht
Museum

Egelantiersgracht

Sint-Andrieshof
Leliestraat
**Anne
Frankhuis**

Prinsengracht
Lellegracht
Lellegracht

Nieuwe
Bloemgracht
Bloemgracht
Westerkerk

Bloemgracht
Bloemstraat
Homomonument

Marnixstraat
Wester-
markt

Rozen
ROZENGRACHT
Rozenstraat
Reestraat
Hartenstraat

Laurierstraat
Prinsengracht
Prinsengracht
Keizersgracht
Keizersgracht

Laurierstraat
Laurergracht
Laurergracht

Lijnbaansgracht
Elandsstraat
Elands-
straat
Beren-
straat
Wolven-
straat

Elandsgracht
Elandsgracht
**Houseboat
Museum**

Marnixstraat
Oude Looiersstr
Runstraat
Huidenstraat

Looiersgracht
Looiersgracht
Prinsengracht
Keizersgracht
Keizersgracht

Looiersgracht
Passeerdersstr

Passeerdersstr
Leidsegracht
gracht

**Circus
Elleboog**
Molenpad
Leidse-
Leidse-
gracht

Raamstr
Leidse-

**Paleis van
Justitie**

Korte
Lange
Leidsedwarsstr
Kerkstraat
Prinsengracht

Korte
Leidse-
Leidse-
Leidseplein
Leidsekruisstr
Lange Leidsedwarsstr

0   250 m
0   250 yds

C   **D**   **E**

HAARLEMMER

P

Haarlemmer dijk

Haarlemmerstraat

Oude Brug steeg

Korte Prinsen gracht

HOUTTUINEN

Westerdokskade

Haarlemmer straat

Het Ij

Brouwersgracht

Noordermarkt

W Ind
Huis

straat

Noorderkerk

Prinsengracht

Keizersgracht

Keizersgracht

De Rode
Hoed

Prinsen
straat

Keizersgracht

Keizersgracht

Keizersgracht

Keizersgracht

F

G

Anne Frankhuis

'My greatest wish is to be a journalist, and later on, a famous writer... I'd like to publish a book called 'The Secret Annexe'. It remains to be seen whether I'll succeed, but my diary can serve as a basis.'

Unfilled wish On Thursday 11 May 1944, just under three months before she was captured by the Nazis, Anne Frank wrote these poignant words in her diary. She never saw it published, but died in the concentration camp at Bergen-Belsen near the end of World War II, at age 15.

'The Secret Annexe' After Nazi Germany invaded the Netherlands in 1940, increasingly severe anti-Semitic measures were introduced. In 1942, the Frank and van Daan families went into hiding. For the next two years, Anne Frank kept a diary

Waiting to see inside Anne Frankhuis is a time for reflection (left)
The bookcase that hid the secrect entrance where Anne and her family hid from the Nazis in 1942 (middle)
It is difficult to believe that a family hid behind this plain façade for two years (right)

describing daily life and the families' isolation and fear of discovery—until they were betrayed to the Nazis in 1944. Her father was the only member of the group to survive. In 1947, following her wishes, he published her diary, calling it Het Achterhuis (The Secret Annexe). Today, over half a million visitors annually make their way through the revolving bookcase that conceals the entrance into the small, gloomy rooms so vividly described in the diary. Mementos on the walls include a map showing the Allied armies' advance from Normandy. Pencilled lines mark the children's growth. The building is preserved by the Anne Frank Foundation, founded to combat racism and anti-Semitism and to promote 'the ideals set down in the Diary of Anne Frank'. In one entry Anne wrote: 'I want to go on living even after my death!' Thanks to her diary, this wish, at least, came true.

THE BASICS

www.annefrank.nl

➕ E4

✉ Prinsengracht 267

☎ 5567105

🕐 Mid-Mar to mid-Sep daily 9–9; mid-Sep to mid-Mar 9–7 (4 May 9–7, 21 and 31 Dec 9–5, 25 Dec 12–5, 1 Jan 12–7)

🚊 Tram 13, 14, 17

🚤 Museumboat stop 7

♿ None

💷 Expensive

❓ 5-minute introductory film

Houseboat Museum

Once a working barge, the Houseboat Museum is a unique insight into life aboard

THE BASICS

www.houseboatmuseum.nl

✚ D5

✉ Prinsengracht opposite No. 296, facing Elandsgracht

☎ 4270750

🕐 Mar–end Oct Wed–Sun 11–5; Nov–end Feb Fri–Sun 11–5. Closed 1 Jan, 30 Apr, 25, 26, 31 Dec

🍴 Café

🚊 Tram 13, 14, 17

♿ None

💶 Inexpensive

HIGHLIGHTS

● Browsing the houseboat library
● Watching the slide show
● Sipping coffee in the café corner at the same eye level as the ducks

Some 2,500 houseboats line the canals of Amsterdam, homes to people who prefer the alternative lifestyle of being afloat. The Houseboat Museum explores the appeal of a floating home.

Home from home This museum—Woonbootmuseum in Dutch—feels exactly like someone's home, and the question that visitors most often ask is whether somebody still lives aboard the *Hendrika Maria*, a retired canal barge built in 1914. In fact, nobody does, but visitors are invited to pretend that they do: In this museum you are allowed to make yourself at home, sit in the comfortable armchairs and browse the books that line the walls of the surprisingly spacious living area.

High maintenance Another common reaction is: 'I'd love to live on a boat like this'. The museum provides plenty of information about houseboat living to encourage such dreams but warns about the rising price of moorings in Amsterdam. The slide show makes it clear that maintaining a houseboat is a work of love. Every three to four years the boat has to be taken out of the water and pressure hosed to remove corrosive accretions. Loose rivets have to be replaced and even whole sections of hull if they become thin.

Rising costs When all the costs are added up, houseboat living is not substantially cheaper than living in an equivalent-size apartment. But people who live on boats are passionate and would not have it any other way.

The handsome Princes' Canal (left) with its fine buildings including the Westertoren (right)

Prinsengracht

Of the three canals that form the Grachtengordel (Canal Ring), Prinsengracht is in many ways the most atmospheric, with its fine merchants' homes, converted warehouses and flower-laden houseboats.

Prince William's canal Prinsengracht (Prince's Canal), named after William of Orange, was dug at the same time as Herengracht and Keizersgracht as part of a massive 17th-century expansion scheme. Together these three form the city's distinctive horseshoe-shaped canal network. Less exclusive than the other two waterways, with smaller houses, Prinsengracht became an important thoroughfare lined with warehouses and merchants' homes. Cargo would be unloaded from ships into fourth-floor storehouses by means of the massive hoist-beams seen today in the gables of many buildings (and still used for lifting furniture). Some houses were built with a deliberate tilt, to protect their façades from the goods as they were hoisted.

Floating homes Today, you'll also see some of Amsterdam's most beautiful houseboats, some with gardens, moored along Prinsengracht, near Brouwersgracht and alongside the ivy-covered quays close to the Amstel. Amsterdammers have long lived on houseboats, but the housing crisis after World War II skyrocketed the population of boat-people, so that there are more than 2,500 legal houseboats in Amsterdam, all with a postal address and power hook-ups. The unofficial figure is a lot higher.

THE BASICS

🔳 E3
🍴 Bars, cafés, restaurants
🚊 Tram 1, 2, 4, 5, 6, 13, 14, 16, 17, 24, 25
🚤 Museumboat stop 7

HIGHLIGHTS

● Amstelkerk (▷ 75)
● Anne Frankhuis (▷ 24–25)
● Noorderkerk (▷ 30)
● Noordermarkt (▷ 30)
● Westerkerk (▷ 28)

DID YOU KNOW?

● Prinsengracht is 4.5km (3 miles) long, 2m (6ft) deep and 25m (80ft) wide to accommodate four lanes of shipping.
● A law (dating from 1565) restricts the lean of canal houses to 1:25.

THE WEST

TOP 25

Westerkerk

TOP 25

The view from the church's clock tower, topped with a stunning crown, is panoramic

THE BASICS

www.westerkerk.nl

➕ E4

✉ Prinsengracht 281, Westermarkt

☎ Church 6247766, tower 6126856

🕐 Church Apr–end Sep Mon–Fri 11–3; tower Apr–end Sep Mon–Fri 10–5. Times can vary and church may be closed at times stated

🚊 Tram 13, 14, 17

🚢 Museumboat stop 7

♿ Few

🎫 Inexpensive (tower)

❓ Carillon concerts most Tue at noon

HIGHLIGHTS

● Climbing the tower
● Organ, Johannes Duyschot (1686)
● Anne Frank statue, Mari Andriessen
● Rembrandt memorial column
● Grave of Rembrandt's son, Titus

This is the most beautiful of the four churches built in the 17th century to the north, south, east and west of the city's core. The views from the tall tower are unsurpassable and make the 85m (280ft) climb worthwhile.

Masterwork The West Church, the church most visited by tourists in the city, has the largest nave of any Dutch Protestant church, and the tallest tower and largest congregation in Amsterdam. It is the masterwork of Dutch architect Hendrick de Keyser, who died in 1621, one year after construction began. Designed to serve the wealthy bourgeoisie living in the stylish new mansions of the Canal Ring, it was eventually completed by his son Pieter with Cornelis Dancker in 1631. To its tower they added the gaudy golden crown—a symbol of the city granted by Habsburg Emperor Maximilian 150 years earlier. The sweeping views over the Prinsengracht gables can be seen from the tower, popularly called 'Lange Jan' (Tall John). Outside the church, people often lay wreaths at the foot of the statue of Anne Frank, who used to listen to the church carillon while she was in hiding, before the bells were melted down by the Nazis.

Interior The simple, whitewashed interior is laid out in the shape of a double Greek cross. The massive organ is decorated with musical instruments and frescoes of the Evangelists by Gerard de Lairesse, one of Rembrandt's pupils. Rembrandt himself was buried here on 8 October 1669, as was his son, Titus, a year earlier in 1668.

More to See

BLOEMGRACHT AND EGELANTIERSGRACHT
Narrow canals in the Jordaan, a retreat from the bustle of downtown, lined with pretty, small boats.
🔢 D4 🚊 Tram 13, 14, 17

BROUWERSGRACHT
Stretching from the Canal Ring into the Jordaan, the Brouwersgracht owes its name to the many breweries established here in the 16th and 17th centuries. Houseboats and the old converted warehouses make this leafy canal particularly photogenic.
🔢 E3 🚇 Centraal Station

CIRCUS ELLEBOOG
Learn tightrope walking, juggling and other circus skills at the Elleboog Circus. You need to book.
🔢 D6 ✉ Passeerdersgracht 32
☎ 6269370 🕐 Times vary, call for details
🚊 Tram 7, 10 ♿ Good 💶 Expensive

HOMOMONUMENT
An arresting sculpture is the *Homomonument* (1987) by Dutch artist Karin Daan. Consisting of three pink, granite triangles, the sign homosexuals were forced to wear during the Nazi occupation, it commemorates all those who have been persecuted because of their homosexuality.
🔢 E4 ✉ Corner of Westermarkt and Keizersgracht 🚊 Tram 13, 14, 17

JORDAAN
This popular bohemian quarter with its labyrinth of picturesque canals, narrow streets, trendy shops, cafés and restaurants was once a boggy meadow alongside Prinsengracht. The name is believed to have come from the French *jardin*, meaning garden.
🔢 E3 🚊 Tram 3, 10, 13, 14, 17

KEIZERSGRACHT
Together with Prinsengracht and Herengracht, this broad, elegant canal, built in 1612 and named Emperor's Canal after Emperor Maximilian I, completes the Grachtengordel (Canal Ring)—the trio of concentric central canals.
🔢 E3 🚊 Tram 1, 2, 5, 13, 14, 16, 17, 24

Going to market in the attractive Jordaan district

Try your skills at Circus Elleboog

LEIDSEGRACHT

One of the most exclusive addresses in town.

➕ E6 🚊 Tram 1, 2, 5, 7, 10

LOOIERSGRACHT

In the 17th century, the main industry in the Jordaan was tanning, hence the name Tanner's Canal.

➕ D5 🚊 Tram 7, 10

NOORDERKERK

An austere church, the first in Amsterdam to be constructed in the shape of a Greek cross. It was built in 1620–23 for the Protestant workers in the Jordaan district, and is still well attended. Noorderkerk is the venue for regular classical concerts.

➕ E3 ✉ Noordermarkt 44–48
☎ 6266436 🕐 Sat 11–1, Mon 10.30–1 and services 🚊 Tram 1, 2, 5, 13, 14, 17

NOORDERMARKT

For a taste of the Jordaan district, head for the lively square surrounding the Noorderkerk. On Monday morning visit the Lapjesmarkt textile and second-hand clothing market, and on Saturday try the Boerenmarkt for organic produce, crafts and birds.

➕ E3 ✉ Noordermarkt 🕐 Mon–Fri 9–1, Sat 9–4 🚊 Tram 1, 2, 5, 13, 17

PIANOLA MUSEUM

www.pianola.nl

For something completely different visit the small Pianola Museum. There are nearly 20,000 music rolls in the museum archive, composers such as Mahler, Debussy, Ravel and Strauss recorded in this way. There are concerts in the museum every month.

➕ E3 ✉ Westerstraat ☎ 6279624
🕐 Sun 11.30–5.30. Group tours all week by appointment 🚊 Tram 13, 14, 17

TULIP MUSEUM

www.amsterdamtulipmuseum.com

Close to Anne Frankhuis, this excellent little museum traces the history of the tulip from its origins in Central Asia. Round off your visit in the shop, selling every bulb imaginable.

➕ E4 ✉ Prinsengracht 112 ☎ 4210095
🕐 Tue–Sun 10–6 🚊 Tram 13, 14, 17

Amsterdam is renowned for its beautiful tulips

A Walk into Jordaan

A pleasant stroll from the busy Dam Square to the pretty quiet canals of the west and on through the local district of the Jordaan.

DISTANCE: 4km (2.5 miles) **ALLOW:** 1–2 hours

START

DAM SQUARE
✚ F4 🚊 Tram 4, 9, 14, 16, 24, 25

1 Leave Dam Square via Paleisstraat; continue straight over the scenic Singel, Herengracht and Keizersgracht canals, and then turn right alongside Prinsengracht.

2 Pass Westerkerk (▷ 28) and Anne Frankhuis (▷ 24–25) and turn left on Leliegracht and cross Prinsengracht and double back for a few metres along the bank of the canal.

3 You will reach the peaceful Bloemgracht (▷ 29) canal. Turn right here, take the second right up Tweede Leliedwarsstraat, cross over Egelantiersgracht (▷ 29) and turn right along its shady bank.

4 Turn left up Tweede Egelantiersdwarsstraat into the heart of the bohemian Jordaan district, very much a local suburb with some unusual shops.

END

DAM SQUARE
✚ F4 🚊 Tram 4, 9, 14, 16, 24, 25

8 Continue across Nieuwezijds Voorburgwal, past the magnificent Nieuwe Kerk (▷ 47) on the left and return to the Dam.

7 Cross by the sluice gates and turn right along the eastern side of the Singel, past Amsterdam's narrowest house façade (No. 7). To conclude the walk, turn left at Torensteeg, cross Spui and go along Molensteeg.

6 You come to attractive Brouwersgracht (▷ 29), lined with traditional barges and houseboats. Cross Brouwersgracht at Herengracht and walk along Brouwersgracht to the Singel.

5 Walk on to Lijnbaansgracht, and then turn right into Lindengracht, once a canal.

Shopping

AMSTERDAM SMALLEST GALLERY
An original painting of the city bought here will remind you of your stay.
🕂 E4 ✉ Westermarkt 60 ☎ 6223756 🚊 Tram 13, 14, 17

BEADIES
Do-it-yourself jewellery: Choose from a huge range of vibrant beads to create your own bracelets or necklaces.
🕂 E5 ✉ Huidenstraat 6 ☎ 4285161 🚊 Tram 1, 2, 5, 13, 17

BLUE GOLD FISH
Storehouse of fantastical gifts including jewellery, ornaments, home fixtures, fabrics and more.
🕂 D4 ✉ Rozengracht 17 ☎ 6233134 🚊 Tram 13, 14, 17

CLAIRE V
www.clairev.nl
Gorgeous high-quality hand-woven silk handbags, evening wraps and accessories, many made by landmine victims in Cambodia. Each bag takes some 20 hours to craft. Lovely for gifts.
🕂 D5 ✉ Prinsengracht 234F ☎ 4219000 🚊 Tram 13, 14, 17

CORA KEMPERMAN
Elegant and imaginative, fashionable yet bohemian, individually designed women's fashion.
🕂 E6 ✉ Leidsestraat 72 ☎ 6251284 🚊 Tram 1, 2, 5

CORTINA PAPIER
Stocks all kinds of notebooks, from plain to leather-bound, along with fine paper and writing materials.
🕂 E4 ✉ Reestraat 22 ☎ 6236676 🚊 Tram 6, 13, 14, 17

DREAM LOUNGE
Anything's possible in Amsterdam. This is just one of several shops that specializes in 'magic mushrooms'. Part of the Conscious Dreams group, which also has a tattoo service.
🕂 E6 ✉ Kerkstraat 113 ☎ 6266907 🚊 Tram 1, 2, 5

EICHHOLTZ
Established delicatessen with Dutch, American and English specialties. An expats heaven.
🕂 E6 ✉ Leidsestraat 48 ☎ 6220305 🚊 Tram 1, 2, 5

SHOPPING TIPS

Although Amsterdam does not compare with Paris or London for European chic, the large number of unusual specialist shops, second-hand shops and vibrant markets among its more than 10,000 shops and department stores, make shopping a real pleasure. Interesting souvenirs and gifts to take home are easy to find, whatever your budget. For shopping with a difference and a certain individuality, Amsterdam is hard to beat.

DE FIETSENMAKER
One of the top bike shops in Amsterdam.
🕂 D5 ✉ Lauriergracht 50 ☎ 6258352 🚊 Tram, 13, 14, 17

FIFTIES-SIXTIES
A jumble of period pieces including toasters, vacuum cleaners records, lamps and other mementos of this hip era.
🕂 E4 ✉ Reestraat 5 ☎ 6232653 🚊 Tram 13, 14, 17

FROZEN FOUNTAIN
www.frozenfountain.nl
Not only is this striking interiors shop a dazzling showcase for up-and-coming Dutch designers, it is a fabulous place for finding unusual gifts, ceramics and jewellery.
🕂 E5 ✉ Prinsengracht 645 ☎ 622 9375 🚊 Tram 1, 2, 5

GALLERIA D'ARTE RINASCIMENTO
For all kinds, and quality, of Delftware, from the most expensive products of De Porcelyne Fles to cheap souvenirs, this piled-high shop also sells excellent polychrome Makkumware.
🕂 E4 ✉ Prinsengracht 170 ☎ 6227509 🚊 Tram 13, 14, 17

HEINEN HANDPAINTED DELFTWARE
Tiny but delightful for its Delftware plates, tulip vases and beautiful Christmas decorations.

📍 E6 ✉ Prinsengracht 440
☎ 6278299 🚋 Tram 1, 2, 5, 5, 13, 17

J. G. BEUNE
Famous for chocolate versions of *Amsterdammertjes* (the posts lining the streets to prevent cars parking on the pavement), and a mouth-watering array of cakes and sweets.
📍 E2 ✉ Haarlemmerdijk 156 ☎ 6248356 🚋 Tram 1, 2, 5, 13, 17

JORDINO
Gorgeous creations in marzipan or chocolate, plus home-made ice cream.
📍 E2 ✉ Haarlemmerdijk 25a ☎ 4203225 🚋 Tram 1, 2, 5, 13, 17

DE KINDER-BOEKWINKEL
Children's books, arranged according to age.
📍 D4 ✉ Rozengracht 34 ☎ 6224761 🚋 Tram 13, 14, 17

KITSCH KITCHEN SUPERMERCADO
www.kitschkitchen.nl
Ghanaian metal furniture, Indian bead curtains, Mexican tablecloths, Chinese pots and pans—the whole world in one bright kitchen! An amazing variety of goods on sale including masses of plastic.
📍 D4 ✉ Rozengracht 8–12 ☎ 6228261 🚋 Tram 13, 14, 17

LAMBIEK
www.lambiek.net
The world's oldest comic shop. Huge selection from around the world in many languages.
📍 E6 ✉ Kerkstraat 132 ☎ 6267543 🚋 Tram 1, 2, 5

DE LOOIER KUNST- & ANTIEKCENTRUM
A covered antiques market with hundreds of stalls selling everything from quality items to junk. Open Saturday to Thursday 11–5.
📍 D5 ✉ Elandsgracht 109 ☎ 6249038 🚋 Tram 7, 10, 17

OUTRAS COISAS
Stylish furniture and furnishings for every room of your home. You will find products from the traditional to the contemporary to choose from as well as handmade

OFFBEAT SHOPS
Tiny specialist shops and boutiques selling everything from psychedelic mushrooms to designer soap and kitsch toilet furniture can be found all over the city. Many are in the Jordaan and along the web of sidestreets that connect the ring canals between Leidsegracht and Brouwersgracht.
Explore the second-hand shops of the Jordaan for a bargain, or sift through local street markets. Shopping in Amsterdam is fun.

pottery, hand-blown glass, jewellery and a large collection of handbags.
📍 E3 ✉ Herenstraat 31 ☎ 6257281 🚋 Tram 1, 2, 5, 13, 17

LA SAVONNERIE
A veritable pot-pourri of bathtime products and accessories. You can even have your own personal text inscribed on the delicious handmade soaps.
📍 D5 ✉ Prinsengracht 294 ☎ 4281139 🚋 Tram 13, 14, 17

SHIRDAK
www.shirdak.nl
For something a bit different and for lovers of eastern textiles, try this interesting shop promoting products from Central Asia. Slippers, rugs, gifts, all in gorgeous hues. Also European felt hats, each one a unique design and a work of art.
📍 D4 ✉ Prinsengracht 192 ☎ 6266800 🚋 Tram 13, 14, 17

SISSY-BOY
www.sissy-boy.nl
Popular Dutch clothing chain with stylish, affordable clothing for men and women.
📍 E6 ✉ Leidsestraat 15 ☎ 6238949 🚋 Tram 1, 2, 5

DE WITTE TANDENWINKEL
Just about everything you could want for your teeth.
📍 E5 ✉ Runstraat 5 ☎ 6233443 🚋 Tram 1, 2, 5, 13, 14, 16, 17, 24

Entertainment and Nightlife

ALTO JAZZ CAFÉ
One of Amsterdam's best jazz and blues venues. Live music nightly, pricey drinks.

➕ E6 ✉ Korte Leidsedwarsstraat 115 ☎ 6263249 🚊 Tram 1, 2, 5, 7, 10

BAMBOO BAR
Tiny, dark and smoky, this atmospheric bar plays excellent live music nightly—jazz, rhythm and blues and salsa. Popular for its world music, too.

➕ E6 ✉ Lange Leidsedwarsstraat 64 ☎ 6243993 🚊 Tram 1, 2, 5, 7, 10

BOURBON STREET
www.bourbonstreet.nl
Nightly blues and jazz. Friendly staff create a good atmosphere. Love of good music brings fans of all ages and expect to see some famous names.

➕ E6 ✉ Leidsekruisstraat 6–8 ☎ 6233440 🚊 Tram 7, 10

BRASIL MUSIC BAR
www.brazilmusicbar.com
Brazilian bar with live salsa on Wednesday nights from 11pm to 4am.

➕ E6 ✉ Lange Leidsedwarsstraat 70 ☎ 6261500 🚊 Tram 1, 2, 5, 6, 7, 10

FELIX MERITIS
www.felixmeritis.nl
An important avant-garde dance and drama revue, and home to the Felix Meritis experimental theatre company.

➕ E5 ✉ Keizersgracht 324 ☎ 6231311 reservations; 6262321 general information 🚊 Tram 13, 14, 17

HET LAND VAN WALEM
One of Amsterdam's first modern bars, still tolerably trendy after all these years.

➕ F6 ✉ Keizersgracht 449 ☎ 6253544 🚊 Tram 1, 2, 5

HET MOLENPAD
An old-fashioned brown café. The canalside terrace catches the early evening sun.

➕ E6 ✉ Prinsengracht 653 ☎ 6259680 🚊 Tram 1, 2, 5

LUXEMBOURG
Watch the world go by over canapés or colossal club sandwiches on the terrace of this elegant, high-ceiling bar.

➕ E5 ✉ Spui 24 ☎ 6206264 🚊 Tram 1, 2, 5

MAZZO
A young image-conscious crowd prop up the bar of this small but chic disco in the Jordaan, while guest DJs and live bands play the latest sounds to keep things lively.

➕ D4 ✉ Rozengracht 114 ☎ 6267500 🕐 Thu–Sun 11pm–5am 🚊 Tram 13, 14, 17

PAPENEILAND
Amsterdam's oldest bar has retained its old-world charm with panelled walls, Makkum tiles, candles, benches and a comforting wood-burning stove.

➕ E3 ✉ Prinsengracht 2 ☎ 6241989 🚊 Tram 1, 2, 5, 13, 17

DE PRINS
Very much a locals' bar, despite its proximity to the Anne Frankhuis, with a cosy pub atmosphere and seasonal menu.

➕ E4 ✉ Prinsengracht 124 ☎ 6249382 🚊 Tram 13, 14, 17

DE TWEE ZWAANTJES
Traditional Dutch entertainment off the tourist track in a tiny bar full of accordion-playing, folk-singing Jordaaners.

➕ E4 ✉ Prinsengracht 114 ☎ 6252729 🕐 Thu–Tue 🚊 Tram 13, 14, 17, 20

ANCIENT AND MODERN
Brown cafés, so-called because of their chocolate painted walls and dark wooden fittings, are reminiscent of the interiors in Dutch old master paintings. Here you can meet the locals in a setting that's *gezellig* (cosy). In stark contrast, there are a growing number of brasserie-like grand cafés, and chic, modern bars with stylish, spacious interiors. Watch also for the tiny ancient *proeflokalen* tasting bars (originally distillers' private sampling rooms), serving a host of gins and liqueurs.

Restaurants

ALBATROS (€€–€€€)
Eschews the fancy demeanour affected by many seafood eateries, preferring to rely on its homey neighbourhood style and great-tasting seafood.
➕ D3 ✉ Westerstraat 264, Jordaan ☎ 6279932
🕐 Daily lunch, dinner
🚃 Tram 3, 10

DE BELHAMEL (€€)
Art nouveau and classical music set the tone for polished Continental cuisine in an intimate, often crowded setting with a superb canal view.
➕ E3 ✉ Brouwersgracht 60, Jordaan ☎ 6221095
🕐 Dinner only 🚃 Tram 1, 2, 5, 6, 13, 17

DE BLAUWE HOLLANDER (€)
Generous portions of wholesome and modestly priced fare in a lively bistro setting.
➕ E6 ✉ Leidsekruisstraat 28, Grachtengordel
☎ 6233014 🕐 Daily lunch, dinner 🚃 Tram 1, 2, 5, 7, 10

BOJO (€€)
www.bojo.nl
Popular late-night eatery serving huge portions of rice and noodle dishes and delicious satays. If you're hungry this is the place with good size portions, and plenty of vegetarian choices too.
➕ E6 ✉ Lange Leidsedwarsstraat 51, Grachtengordel ☎ 6227434
🕐 Mon–Fri dinner, Sat–Sun lunch, dinner 🚃 Tram 1, 2, 5, 7, 10

DE BOLHOED (€)
A trendy restaurant on the edge of the Jordaan, with vegetarian pâtés, salads and hearty vegan dishes.
➕ E3 ✉ Prinsengracht 60-62, Grachtengordel
☎ 6261803 🕐 Daily lunch, dinner 🚃 Tram 13, 14, 17

CHRISTOPHE (€€€)
Chef Jean-Christophe Royer combines French style and US experience to great effect in his chic canalside restaurant.

➕ E4 ✉ Leliegracht 46, Jordaan ☎ 6250807
🕐 Mon–Sat dinner only
🚃 Tram 6, 13, 14, 17, 20

CINEMA PARADISO (€€)
Spacious restaurant attracting the cool crowd and serving good honest Italian fare.
➕ D3 ✉ Westerstraat 186, Jordaan ☎ 6237344
🕐 Tue–Sun dinner from 6pm
🚃 Tram 3, 10

THE DYLAN RESTAURANT (€€€)
This superior restaurant in the elegant Dylan hotel (▷ 112) is renowned for its blending of both classic and contemporary cuisine from east and west. Open for lunch, dinner and afternoon tea.
➕ E5 ✉ Keizersgracht 384, Grachtengordel ☎ 5302010
🕐 Daily lunch, dinner
🚃 Tram 1, 2, 5

GARY'S MUFFINS (€)
Fresh-filled bagels, muffins and brownies. A good value snack.
➕ F7 ✉ Prinsengracht 454, Grachtengordel ☎ 4201452
🕐 Daily lunch, dinner
🚃 Tram 1, 2, 5, 13, 17

GELATERIA JORDINO (€)
Bright and breezy place that does great homemade Italian ice cream and waistline-threatening chocolate cake.
➕ E2 ✉ Haarlemmerdijk 25, Centrum ☎ 4203225
🕐 Daily 10–8 🚃 Bus 18, 22

DE GROENE LANTAARN (€€)

www.fondue.nl

This tiny restaurant on a quiet leafy canal, specializes in Gouda fondues.

➕ D4 ✉ Bloemgracht 47, Jordaan ☎ 6202088
🕐 Thu–Sun dinner only
🚋 Tram 13, 14, 17

MOEDER'S POT (€)

No frills food served at communal tables; chunky soups, casseroles, mussels, chicken and ham. No credit cards.

➕ E2 ✉ Vinkenstraat 119, Jordaan ☎ 6237643
🕐 Mon–Sat 5–9.30
🚋 Tram 10

PANCAKE BAKERY (€)

www.pancake.nl

The best pancakes in town, and a good place to take the children with a choice of some 50 types of pancake. In the basement of an old canal house, it's a nice setting but you do need to like pancakes as there's really not much else.

➕ E4 ✉ Prinsengracht 191, Grachtengordel ☎ 6251333
🕐 Daily 🚋 Tram 13, 14, 17

POMPADOUR (€)

The finest chocolatier in town doubles as a sumptuous tearoom. The tiny Louis XVI-style *salon de thé* is the perfect setting to eat your incredibly rich chocolate cakes.

➕ E5 ✉ Huidenstraat 12, Grachtengordel ☎ 6239554
🕐 Mon–Sat 9–6 🚋 Tram 1, 2, 5

RESTAURANT BLOESEM (€€)

www.restaurantbloesem.nl

In a relaxed, informal yet chic atmosphere, there are two dining areas in this restaurant interconnected by arches. Choose from meat, game—try quail filled with red onion and pancetta or basil—fish or vegetarian dishes such as marinated eggplant with mozarella.

➕ E2 ✉ Binnen Dommersstraat 13, Jordaan ☎ 7700407 🕐 Dinner only from 5pm 🚋 Tram 7, 10, 16, 24, 25

SHERPA (€)

www.sherpa-restaurant.nl

Nepalese/Tibetan venue with traditional Himalayan ornaments. Nepalese meals are spicy; Tibetan are prepared with noodles and ravioli.

➕ E6 ✉ Korte Leidsedwarsstraat 58,

DUTCH SUSHI

Long before Japanese sushi became fashionable fast food in Europe, the Low Countries already had their own version—raw herring—accompanied by chopped onion and pickles. Be sure to try some at one of the herring stalls dotted around town. Kromhout (✉ at the junction of Singel and Raadhuisstraat), and Volendammer Viswinkel (✉ le van der Helststraat 60) are considered by locals as two of the best.

Grachtengordel ☎ 6239495
🕐 Dinner only (lunch in summer) 🚋 Tram 1, 2, 5, 6, 7, 10

TOSCANINI (€€)

The best Italian food in town. You need to reserve well ahead.

➕ E3 ✉ Lindengracht 75, Jordaan ☎ 6232813
🕐 Mon–Sat dinner only
🚋 Tram 3

VAN PUFFELEN (€€)

A classic brown café that happens to to be a good restaurant too. Wholesome French-style cooking is served in the lovely panelled dining room.

➕ E5 ✉ Prinsengracht 375–377, Grachtengordel ☎ 6246270 🕐 Mon–Fri 6pm–11pm, Sat–Sun 12–5, 6–11 🚋 Tram 13, 14, 17, 20

DE VLIEGENDE SCHOTEL (€€)

www.vliegendeschotel.com

Filling soups, salads, noodles and *rijsttafels* are on the menu at 'The Flying Saucer'. With generous portions, it makes this place worth a visit.

➕ D4 ✉ Nieuwe Leliestraat 162–168, Jordaan
☎ 6252041 🕐 Daily 4pm–10.45pm 🚋 Tram 10

WINKEL (€)

A popular café by the Noordermarkt. A great spot for people-watching when the markets are open.

➕ E3 ✉ Noordermarkt 43, Jordaan ☎ 6230223
🕐 Closed Sat, Mon lunch
🚋 Tram 3, 10

This is the heart of Amsterdam, the tourist hub with its main shopping streets and upfront brashness of the Red Light District. Yet here, too, are medieval buildings, pretty canals and oases of calm and solitude.

Het Ij

DE RUIJTERKADE

CENTRAAL
STATION

stationsplein

HENDRIK-

The Ij

Sint-
Nicolaaskerk

Oosterdokskade

Schreierstoren

Nieuwbrug

Zeedijk

Oudezijds
Kolk

KADE

Oosterdokskade

Museum
Amstelkring

Geldersekade

Lange
Niezel

Zeedijk

Korte
Niezel

Oude
Kerk

Fo Guang Shan
He Hua Temple

Voorburgwal

Voorburgwal

CHINATOWN

Achterburgwal

Achterburgwal

Nieuw-
markt

Oudezijds
Achterburgwal

Oude
Hoogstr.

Kloveniersburgwal

Kloveniersburgwal

G

H

Amsterdams Historisch Museum

TOP 25

HIGHLIGHTS

● *View of Amsterdam*, Cornelis Anthonisz (1538), the oldest city map
● *The First Steamship on the IJ*, Nicolaas Bauo (1816)
● *Girls from the Civic Orphanage*, Nicolaas van der Waay (1880)
● Bell room

TIPS

● Make sure you get a plan of the musem as it can be easy to get lost without one.
● Browse the souvenir shop.

Do make this lively and informative museum your first port of call. Once you have a grasp of Amsterdam's rich history, walking around the city is all the more rewarding.

The building This excellent museum traces the growth of Amsterdam from 13th-century fishing village to bustling metropolis, through an impressive collection of paintings, maps, models and historical objects. They are displayed chronologically in one of the city's oldest buildings. Originally a monastery, it was occupied by the city orphanage (Burgerweeshuis) for nearly 400 years, until 1975, when it was converted into a museum. Most of the present structure dates from the 16th and 17th centuries. Throughout, you can still see evidence of its former use—notably the ceiling

Detail from a plaque in the Amsterdams Historisch Museum (far left). The former Burgerweeshuis for orphans, now the entrance to the musem (left). 19th-century pharmacy sign (right). Market scene by P. Pietersz, 1610 (below left). Brass weights and scales on display at the museum (below middle). Suits of armour (below right)

paintings in the Regent's Chamber and the numerous portraits of children, including Jan Carel van Speyck, who later became a Dutch naval hero.

The collections The first rooms of the museum chronicle the city's early history and its rise to prominence in trade and commerce. The displays include furniture, memorabilia and a map that illuminates each 25-year period of growth through the centuries. The museum's main focus is on the Golden Age and colonial expansion. Paintings and photographs illustrate the growing welfare problems of the 19th and early 20th centuries, and a small collection of relics from World War II shows how the Nazi occupation affected the city's population, 10 per cent of which was Jewish. A section focuses on the 'Modern City'. There are portraits of the Civic Guard in the adjoining Schuttersgalerij.

THE BASICS

www.ahm.nl

⊞ F5

✉ Kalverstraat 92, Nieuwezijds Voorburgwal 357, Sint-Luciënsteeg 27

☎ 5231822

🕓 Mon–Fri 10–5, Sat–Sun 11–5. Closed 1 Jan, 30 Apr, 25 Dec

🍴 David and Goliath Café

🚋 Tram 1, 2, 4, 5, 9, 14, 16, 24, 25

♿ Good

💷 Expensive

❓ Guided tours on request: call in advance—takes one hour

Begijnhof

The beautifully pre-served buildings of the Begijnhof provided a sanctuary of peace

THE BASICS

www.begijnjhofamsterdam.nl

⊞ E5

✉ Gedempte Begijnensloot, entrance in Spui

🕓 Daily 9–5, enter chapel after 5pm via gate in Spui

🚊 Tram 1, 2, 5

♿ Good

💵 Free

❓ Shop

DID YOU KNOW?

● The last Begijn died in 1971.

● The Pilgrim Fathers are said to have worshipped here before crossing the Atlantic in the *Mayflower*.

● Today, the Begijnhof is a residence for single women earning less than €16,000 a year, and has a 5-year waiting list.

Tranquillity characterizes the city's many *hofjes* (almshouses), none more so than this leafy oasis. The cobbled courtyard looks like a film set.

Pious women A tiny, unlikely looking gateway leads to the Begijnhof, the oldest and finest *hofje* in the country (almshouses were charitable lodgings for the poor). This secluded community of magnificently restored old houses and gardens clustered around a small church lies a stone's throw from the main shopping thoroughfare. It was built in 1346 as a sanctuary for the Begijnen or Beguines, unmarried women who wanted to live in a religious community without becoming nuns. In return for modest lodging, they devoted themselves to the care of the poor and sick.

Two churches The Begijnkerk (1419), dominating the courtyard, was confiscated from the Beguines during the Protestant Alteration in 1578. The women continued to worship secretly until religious tolerance was restored about 200 years later, in 1795. Meanwhile, their precious church became a warehouse until 1607, when it was given to the city's Scottish Presbyterian community and renamed (or misnamed) the Engelse Kerk (English Church). The simple interior has pulpit panels by Piet Mondrian. Nearby, Het Houten Huys (The Wooden House, 1425) is one of only two remaining wood-fronted houses in Amsterdam. It was built before 1521, when the use of wood as a building material was banned, after a series of fires.

Not just tulips in Amsterdam, the Bloememarkt has all kinds of plants on offer

Bloemenmarkt

Golden sunflowers, deep blue irises, delicately scented roses and row upon row of tulips and tulip bulbs—a vibrant blaze on the floating stalls of the flower market.

Floating market During the 17th and 18th centuries there were approximately 20 floating markets in Amsterdam, at least two of which gratified the Dutch passion for tulips. Nurserymen would sail up the Amstel from their smallholdings and moor here to sell their wares directly from their boats. Today, the stalls at this, the city's only remaining floating market, are permanently moored—and not all of the sales space is actually afloat. Offering a vast variety of seasonal flowers, plants, pots, shrubs and herbs, they are supplied by the florists of Aalsmeer and the region around Haarlem, at the horticultural heart of Holland. Over 16,000ha (39,540 acres) of the country are devoted to bulb growing.

Tulip mania Tulips were first spotted in Turkey by Dutch diplomats, who brought them back to Holland around 1600. Shortly afterwards, a Leiden botanist discovered ways of changing their shape and hue, and tulip cultivation rapidly became a national obsession. Prices soared, with single bulbs fetching up to €1,360 (an average worker's annual salary was €68). Some were even exchanged for houses, and an abundance of still life paintings was produced to capture prize blooms on canvas. In 1637, the bubble burst, and many people lost entire fortunes. Prices are more realistic today and tulip bulbs are popular souvenirs for tourists.

THE BASICS

➕ F6
✉ Singel, between Muntplein and Koningsplein
🕐 Mon–Fri 9–6, Sat 9–5
🚇 Muntplein
🚋 Tram 1, 2, 4, 5, 9, 14, 16, 24, 25
🚤 Museumboat stop 4
♿ Good

HIGHLIGHTS

● The sights and smells are worth braving the crowds
● The best variety of tulips in the city as well as other types of plants and bulbs
● Decorative wooden tulips

Herengracht

Houses of all shapes and sizes, and with intricate gables, line the banks of Herengracht

HIGHLIGHTS

● No. 43–45: Oldest warehouses (1600)
● No. 168–172: Theatre Museum and Bartolotti Huis
● No. 366: Bible Museum
● No. 409–411: 'Twin brothers' facing the 'twin sisters' (No. 390–392)
● No. 475: 'Jewel of Canal Houses'
● No. 497: Kattenkabinet (cat museum)
● No. 502: House of Columns (mayor's residence)
● No. 605: Museum Willet-Holthuysen (▷ 71)

DID YOU KNOW?

● If you stand on the bridge at the junction of Herengracht and Reguliersgracht, you can see 15 bridges simultaneously.

Exploring the city's grandest canal is like going back through time to Amsterdam's Golden Age. These gilded houses display four centuries of Dutch architectural styles.

The Gentlemen's Canal Herengracht takes its name from the rich merchants and traders of Amsterdam's heyday, and was the first of three concentric canals dug early in the 17th century to house the city's fast-growing population. Attracting the wealthiest merchant aristocrats, it has the largest, most ostentatious houses, 400 of which are now protected monuments. The houses had to conform to many building standards. Even the tone of the front doors—known as Amsterdam green—was regulated. As on all canals, taxes were levied according to the width of the canal frontage, hence the rows of tall, narrow residences.

Gable-spotting Canal house-owners expressed themselves in the elaborate decoration of their houses' gables and façades. The earliest and most common are the step gable and the spout gable. Amsterdam's first neck gable (No. 168) was built in 1638 by Philips Vingboons, and the bell gable became popular early in the 18th century. Around this time, Louis XIV-style façades were considered the height of fashion. No. 475 is a fine example— named the jewel of canal houses.

The Golden Bend Amsterdam's most extravagant mansions, with double fronts, were built between Leidsestraat and Vijzelstraat, along the stretch of the canal since dubbed the 'Golden Bend'.

Koninklijk Paleis

The 17th-century Royal Palace, designed by Jacob van Campen, dominates Dam Square

Don't be put off by the Royal Palace's sober exterior. It belies the lavish decoration inside—a reminder of the wealth of Amsterdam in its heyday.

Civic pride At the height of the Golden Age, architect Jacob van Campen was commissioned to design Europe's largest and grandest town hall, and its classical design was a startling and progressive departure from the Dutch Renaissance style. The poet Constantijn Huygens called the Stadhuis 'the world's Eighth Wonder' and to this day it remains the city's only secular building on such a grand scale. Note the façade's astonishing wealth of decoration, numerous statues, an elaborate pediment and a huge cupola crowned by a galleon weather vane. During the seven years of construction, a heated argument developed as to whether a tower for the Nieuwe Kerk should have priority over a town hall. This was resolved when the old town hall burned down, and in 1655 the mayor moved into his new building.

Palatial wonder The town hall was transformed into a royal palace in 1808 after Napoleon made his brother Louis King of Holland. Today it serves as an occasional residence for Queen Beatrix, whose principal palace is in The Hague. The Tribunal, within the palace, was once the city's main courtroom, and condemned prisoners were taken from here to be hanged publicly on the Dam. This square has recently been pedestrianized and is a meeting place for locals and tourists, with the palace the major feature.

THE BASICS

www.koninklijkhuis.nl

✚ F4

✉ Nieuwezijds Voorburgwal 147, Dam

☎ 6204060

🕐 Closed for refurbishment until early 2008

🚊 Tram 1, 2, 4, 5, 6, 9, 13, 14, 16, 17, 24, 25

♿ Good

💶 Moderate

HIGHLIGHTS

● Views of the Dam
● Tribunal
● Citizen's Hall
● Façade

DID YOU KNOW?

● The state bought the palace in 1936 for €4.5 million.
● It is 80m (265ft) long and 56m (125ft) wide.
● The bell tower is 51m (119ft) high.

Museum Amstelkring

Golden candle lamp (left) and the beautiful clandestine church of the museum (right)

THE BASICS

www.museum amstelkring.nl

✚ G4

✉ Oudezijds Voorburgwal 40

☎ 6246604

🕐 Mon–Sat 10–5, Sun, public hols 1–5. Closed 1 Jan, 30 Apr

🚉 Centraal Station

🚋 Tram 4, 9, 16, 24, 25

🚉 Centraal Station

⛴ Museumboat stop 1

♿ None

💷 Moderate

❓ Occasional classical concerts in winter

HIGHLIGHTS

● Church of 'Our Dear Lord in the Attic'
● Altar painting *The Baptism of Christ*, Jacob de Wit (1716)
● Priest's bedroom
● Confessional
● Drawing room
● Kitchen

Not only is this tiny museum one of the city's most surprising, it is also tucked away in a small, inconspicuous canal house close to the Red Light District.

Best-kept secret In 1578, when the Roman Catholic city council was replaced by a Protestant one, Roman Catholic churches were closed throughout the city. In 1661, while Catholic church services were still forbidden, a wealthy merchant named Jan Hartman built a residence on Oudezijds Voorburgwal, and two adjoining houses in Heintje Hoeckssteeg. He ran a sock shop on the ground floor, lived upstairs, rented out the spare rooms in the buildings behind, and cleverly converted the top two floors of the canal house and the attics of all three buildings into a secret Catholic church. Religious freedom only returned with the French occupation in 1795.

Hidden church This *'schuilkerk'* was just one of many clandestine churches that sprang up throughout the city, but it is the only one that has been completely preserved. It was saved from demolition in 1888 by a group of historians called the Amstelkring (Amstel Circle), who nicknamed the church 'Our Dear Lord in the Attic'. To find a three-storey, galleried church at the top of a series of increasingly steep staircases is a surprising experience. Given that there is seating for 200 people, magnificent ecclesiastical statuary, silver, paintings, a collapsible altar and a huge organ, it is hard to believe that the services held here were really secret.

Overlooking Dam Square, Niewe Kerk contains some fine monumental tombs

Considering its turbulent history, it is something of a miracle that Holland's magnificent national church has survived. Hearing its organ is a real treat.

Not so new The 'New' Church actually dates from the 15th century, when Amsterdam was growing at such a rate that the 'Old' Church (Oude Kerk, ▷ 48) was no longer sufficient. Construction started in 1408 but the church was several times destroyed by fire. After the Alteration in 1578 (when Amsterdam officially became Protestant), and a further fire in 1645, the church was rebuilt and reconsecrated in 1648. It has no spire: Following years of debate, the money designated for its construction was spent to complete the neighbouring Stadhuis (Town Hall), which is now the Koninklijk Paleis (▷ 45). It does have one of the finest of Amsterdam's 42 historic church organs—a Schonat-Hagerbeer organ, dating 1650–73, with 5,005 pipes and a full-voiced sound that easily fills the church's vast interior.

Famous names At the time of the Alteration, Amsterdam's churches were largely stripped of their treasures, and the Nieuwe Kerk was no exception. The altar space has since been occupied by the tomb of Holland's most valiant naval hero, Admiral Michiel de Ruyter, one of many names from Dutch history, including poets Peter Cornelisz Hooft and Joost van den Vondel. Dutch monarchs have been inaugurated here, from William I in 1815 to Beatrix in 1980. No longer a place of worship, it hosts exhibitions and recitals.

THE BASICS

www.nieuwekerk.nl
🔳 F4
✉ Dam
☎ 6268168
🕐 Usually daily 10–6
🍴 Nieuwe Kafé
🚊 Tram 1, 2, 5, 4, 9, 13, 14, 16, 17, 24, 25
🚢 Museumboat stop 10
♿ Good
🎟 Varies with exhibitions, but mainly expensive
❓ Regular organ concerts, mostly on Sundays. Shop is open daily 10–6, until 10pm on Thu

---

HIGHLIGHTS

● Organ, Hans Schonat and Jacob Hagerbeer (1650–73)
● Organ case, Jacob van Campen (1645)
● Pulpit, Albert Vinckenbrinck (1644)
● Tomb of Admiral de Ruyter, Rombout Verhulst (1681)

Oude Kerk

TOP 25

Dating back to the early 14th century, Oude Kerk is the city's oldest church

THE BASICS

www.oudekerk.nl
✚ F4
✉ Oudekerksplein 23
☎ 6258284
🕐 Mon–Sat 11–5, Sun 1–5.
Closed 1 Jan, 30 Apr, 25 Dec
🚊 Tram 4, 9, 16, 24, 25
♿ Good
⚜ Moderate
❓ Frequent organ recitals and carillon concerts

HIGHLIGHTS

● Great Organ, Vatermüller
● Stained-glass windows, Lambert van Noort (1555)
● Carillon, F. Hemony (1658)
● The tombstone of Rembrandt's first wife, Saskia van Uylenburg, which is still in the church even though poverty drove him to sell her grave plot

Surrounded by cafés, bars and sex shops, the Old Church represents an island of spirituality in the Red Light District. Here brashness and purity rub shoulders.

History Amsterdam's oldest church, dedicated to St. Nicholas, the patron saint of seafarers, was built in 1306 to replace a wooden chapel dating from the late 1200s. Over the centuries the church escaped the great fires that devastated so much of the city, and the imposing basilica you see today dates largely from the 14th century. Its graceful tower, added in 1565–67, contains one of the finest carillons in Holland. In the 16th century Jan Pieters zoon Sweelinck, Holland's best-known composer, was organist here.

Miracle In the 14th century, the Oude Kerk became one of Europe's pilgrimage hubs following a miracle: Communion bread regurgitated by a dying man and thrown on the fire would not burn, and the sick man did not die. Thousands of Catholics still take part in the annual *Stille Omgang* (▷ 114), a silent nocturnal procession, but as the Oude Kerk is now Protestant, it no longer follows the ancient pilgrim route to the church, going instead to the Begijnhof.

Sober interior The stark, impressive interior has a triple nave and elaborate vaulting. Three magnificent windows in the Lady Chapel survived the Alteration, as did the fine choir stalls. In the 1960s some delicate 14th-century paintings were found behind layers of blue paint in the vaults.

You'll see plenty of neon in the Red Light District, Amsterdam's infamous tourist draw

Rosse Buurt

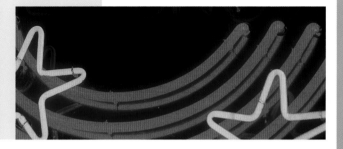

Amsterdam's Red Light District, bathed in a lurid red neon glow, and full of gaping tourists, junkies and pickpockets, is one of the city's greatest attractions.

Sex for sale Because of the port and its sailor population, sex is, and has long been, big business in Amsterdam. As early as the 15th century, Amsterdam was infamous as a haunt of prostitution, and the lure of the Red Light District proves irresistible to curious visitors to the city today. Crowds clog the narrow alleyways, sex shops, peep shows and suggestively named bars, while bored prostitutes beckon from their lighted windows. But there is more to the Red Light District than sex. 'Normal' people live here, too, and go about their everyday business in what, behind the tawdry façade, is an interesting part of the old city.

Drug central The Red Light District is also frequented by drug dealers, and here you will find the great majority of Amsterdam's psychedelic, marijuana-selling 'smoking' coffee shops. The Hash Marihuana Hemp Museum on Oudezijds Achterburgwal traces the history of hashish and the cannabis plant, and is next to the world's only Cannabis Connoisseurs' Club.

Precautions Watch your wallet, avoid eye contact with any undesirable characters, do not take photographs of prostitutes and avoid poorly lighted alleyways. Even though the evening is the liveliest time to visit, don't wander around alone. Be cautious in quiet areas at night, or avoid them completely.

THE BASICS

🔲 F4

✉ Borders roughly denoted by Zeedijk (north), Kloveniersburgwal (east), Damstraat (south) and Warmoesstraat (west)

🍴 Restaurants, bars, cafés

Ⓢ Centraal Station, Nieuwmarkt

🚊 Tram 4, 9, 14, 16, 24, 25

DID YOU KNOW?

● Possession of drugs is technically illegal but the authorities tolerate possession of up to 5g (1oz) of soft drugs (cannabis, hash and marijuana) for personal use.
● Drug-dealing is not allowed. 'Smoking' coffee shops have to be licensed.
● There are some 900 'coffee shops' and 250 cannabis 'grow shops' in Holland, and some 30,000 'home-growers'.
● Brothels were legalized in 1990.
● Half of Amsterdam's prostitutes are foreign.

Singel

The tree-shaded Singel, once the city's first line of defence, is now a residential area

THE BASICS

➕ F4
✉ Singel
☎ Poezenboot 6258794;
www.pozenboot.nl
🕐 Poezenboot daily
1–3pm
🍴 Cafés and restaurants
🚊 Tram 1, 2, 5, 13, 14, 17
🚢 Museumboat stop 4
♿ Poezenboot none
✋ Poezenboot free

HIGHLIGHTS

● Poezenboot
● Bloemenmarkt (▷ 43)
● Torensluis prison cell
● Munttoren (▷ 52)
● No. 7: narrowest house façade
● No. 2, 36, 74, 83: unusual façades

At first glance, this canal looks like any other major waterway in the city. Look a little closer, though, and you will discover some of Amsterdam's most unusual and enchanting sights.

Former city belt From its construction in the early 15th century until the late 16th century, the city limits were marked by the Singel (originally *Cingle*, meaning belt), the city's defensive moat. Then, in 1586, the city council decided to build quays along the Singel's west bank and to convert the moat into a canal for large freight ships. Thus the Singel became the first of Amsterdam's concentric canals, and its curved shape established the horseshoe layout of the city. With the coming of the railways, canal transport became less important and the Singel began to acquire a residential character. Many warehouses are now converted into homes. The Nieuwe Haarlemmersluis, a sluice at the junction of Singel and Brouwersgracht, is opened nightly to top up the city's canals.

All that floats Perhaps the most unusual house is No. 7. The narrowest house front in Amsterdam, it was made no wider than a door in order to minimise property taxes. Opposite is the Poezenboot, a refuge for stray cats. Look out, too, for the Torensluis (Tower Lock, on the Singel's widest bridge); in the 17th century it was used as a prison. The bridge has a monument to Multatuli (1820– 87), one of the Netherlands' greatest writers. The floating flower market, the Bloemenmarkt (which doesn't entirely float), is also on the Singel.

More to See

AMSTERDAM DUNGEON
www.theamsterdamdungeon.nl
The latest of five dungeon attractions to open in Europe and pretty scary too. It's the city's history with the 'horrible' bits. Live shows, actors, a drop ride into hell, a labyrinth and more.
➕ F5 ✉ Rokin 78 ☎ 5308530 🕐 Daily 10.30–6 🚊 Tram 4, 9, 14, 16, 24, 25 💷 Very expensive

BIJBELS MUSEUM
www.bijbelsmuseum.nl
Housed in two historic buildings known as the Cromhouthouses, this museum explores the world through one of the oldest and most read books in the world. You can relax in the lovely garden.
➕ E5 ✉ Herengracht 366–368 ☎ 62424361 🕐 Mon–Sat 10–5, Sun 11–5 🚊 Tram 1, 2, 5 💷 Expensive

BLAUWBURGWAL
Amsterdam's shortest canal extends between Singel and Herengracht, at Herenstraat.
➕ F4 🚊 Tram 1, 2, 5, 6, 13, 17

CENTRAAL STATION
Many visitors get their first glimpse of Amsterdam's architectural wonders at P. J. H. Cuypers' vast Dutch neo-Renaissance station (1889), standing with its back to the IJ harbour.
➕ G3 ✉ Stationsplein 🚇 Centraal Station

CHINATOWN
Amsterdam's 7,000-strong Chinese community earns part of its living from the numerous Chinese restaurants around Nieuwmarkt. The Chinese New Year is celebrated in style here. Take a look at the striking Fo Guang Shan He Hua Temple in Zeedijk, the largest Buddist temple in Europe.
➕ G4 ☎ Temple 4204100 🕐 Temple Mon–Sat 12–5, Sun 10–5; guided tours in English Sat 2, 3, 4 🚇 Nieuwmarkt

FRANCISCUS XAVERIUSKERK
This splendid neo-Gothic church is often dubbed *De Krijtberg* (Chalk Hill), because it is built on the site of a former chalk merchant's house.
➕ E5 ✉ Singel 442–448 ☎ 6231923 🕐 Services only 🚊 Tram 1, 2, 5

The main foyer of Centraal Station

THE IJ

Amsterdam is situated on precariously low-lying ground at the confluence of the IJ (an inlet of the IJsselmeer lake and the Amstel river). During Amsterdam's heyday in the 17th century, most maritime activity was centred on the IJ inlet and along Prins Hendrikkade, where the old warehouses were crammed with exotic produce from the East. Since 1876, access to the sea has been via the North Sea Canal, and the industrial docks are now to the west. The IJ is busy with pleasure boats, barges sailing to and from the port, the free shuttle ferries to Amsterdam-Noord, the paying ferries that connect other points along the waterfront and an occasional warship and visiting cruise liner.

✛ F3 🚊 Centraal Station

MADAME TUSSAUD'S

www.madametussauds.nl

Wax models of Rembrandt, van Gogh, Schwarzenegger and other characters from the 17th century to the present day, and an amazing 5m (16ft) giant clothed in windmills and tulips.

✛ F4 ✉ Dam 20 ☎ 5230623 🕐 Jan–end Oct Mon–Fri, Sun 10–6.30, Sat 10–10; Nov–end Dec daily 10–6.30 🚊 Tram 4, 9, 14, 16, 24, 25 ♿ Good 👋 Very expensive

MUNTTOREN

The tower of the former Mint was part of the southern gateway to the medieval city.

✛ F6 ✉ Muntplein 🚊 Tram 4, 9, 14, 16, 24, 25

NATIONAAL MONUMENT

The 23-m (75-ft) War Memorial obelisk on the Dam contains soil from the then 11 Dutch provinces and the colonies. Every year on 4 May the Queen lays a wreath here.

✛ F4 ✉ Dam 🚊 Tram 4, 9, 14, 16, 24, 25

OUDEMANHUISPOORT

You can find antiquarian bookstalls in this 18th-century arcade, part of the city's university.

✛ F5 ✉ Oudemanhuispoort 🕐 Mon–Fri 11–4 🚊 Tram 1, 2, 5

Dam Square's striking Nationaal Monument

Antiquarian books for sale at Oudemanhuispoort

OUDEZIJDS ACHTERBURGWAL AND OUDEZIJDS VOORBURGWAL

In contrast to most of Amsterdam's canals, which are peaceful and romantic, parts of Oudezijds Achterburgwal and Oudezijds Voorburgwal are lined with glaring, neon-lighted bars and sex shops. The southern sections of both are leafier.

🔁 F5 🚊 Tram 4, 9, 14, 16, 24, 25

POSTZEGELMARKT

A specialist market for stamps, coins and medals.

🔁 E5 ✉ Nieuwezijds Voorburgwal 280
🕙 Wed, Sat 1–4 🚊 Tram 1, 2, 5

SCHREIERSTOREN

The Weeping Tower was where tearful wives and girlfriends waved farewell to their seafaring menfolk. They had good reason to weep: Sailing-ship voyages took up to four years and many sailors died. Today the tower is home to the Café VOC.

🔁 G4 ✉ Prins Hendrikkade 94–95
🚇 Centraal Station

SINT-NICOLAASKERK

Amsterdam's main Roman Catholic church (1888) and one of many Dutch churches named after St. Nicholas, the patron saint of sailors.

🔁 G4 ✉ Prins Hendrikkade 73
☎ 6844803 🕙 Mon–Sat 11–4 and services
🚊 Tram 1, 2, 4, 5, 9, 13, 16, 17, 24, 25

'T LIEVERDJE

In the 1960s this little bronze statue of a boy, which stands so innocently in the middle of the square, became a symbol of the Provo movement, and rallying point of frequent anti-establishment demonstrations. The name means 'Little Rascal'.

🔁 E5 ✉ Spui 🚊 Tram 1, 2, 5

ZEEDIJK

Once the sea wall of the early maritime settlement and until around 1990 a haunt of sailors and shady characters, this area on the fringe of the Red Light District is home to several good bars and restaurants.

🔁 G4 🚇 Centraal Station 🚊 Tram 1, 2, 4, 5, 9, 13, 16, 17, 24, 25

Detail of Schreirstoren, the Weeping Tower

Sint-Nicolaaskerk

Markets and Museums

A walk around the central area of the city, taking in some of the cultural venues, plus a chance to see some markets en route.

DISTANCE: 2km (1 mile) **ALLOW:** 1 hour

START

DAM SQUARE
✚ F4 🚊 Tram 4, 9, 13, 14, 16, 17, 24, 25

END

DAM SQUARE
✚ F4 🚊 Tram 4, 9, 13, 14, 16, 17, 24, 25

❶ Leaving the Dam via Paleisstraat, turn left into Nieuwezijds Voorburgwal, where a stamp and coin market, Postzegelmarkt (▷ 53), is held.

❷ About 100m (100 yards) farther on the left, Sint-Luciënsteeg leads to the excellent and informative Amsterdams Historisch Museum Gallery (▷ 40–41).

❸ Pass through the Schutters-galerij (Civic Guard Gallery) to Gedempte Begijnensloot. At the southern end, a stone archway on your right brings you into the Begijnhof (▷ 42). courtyard.

❹ A further archway leads to Spui. On Friday, stalls sell old books, and on Sundays paintings. Head across the square and turn left along the edge of the Singel (▷ 50).

❽ Ahead of you is the Nationaal Monument (▷ 52), a striking land-mark on Dam Square, bringing you back to the start of your walk.

❼ The museum includes a fine Egyptian collection among its ancient cultural displays. Turn left after the museum over the canal and head first right up busy Rokin, with some antiques shops. At the end, on the left, is Madame Tussaud's (▷ 52).

❻ Your next landmark is the Munttoren (▷ 52) on the left at Muntplein. Cross over the canal (Rokin) and take first left onto Oude Turftmarkt where you will find the Allard Pierson Museum on your right with its collection of antiquities.

❺ Cross the bridge into Koningsplein to the popular flower market, the Bloemenmarkt (▷ 43).

WALK

CENTRAL AMSTERDAM

Shopping

ABSOLUTE DANNY

www.absolutedanny.com
Erotic clothing and accessories with a distinctive design sensibility and a touch of class.

✚ F5 ✉ Oudezijds Achterburgwal 78 ☎ 4210915 Ⓜ Nieuwmarkt

AMERICAN BOOK CENTER

www.abc.nl
Four floors of English-language books, plus US and British magazines and newspapers. Good selection of books on Amsterdam.

✚ F5 ✉ Kalverstraat 185 ☎ 6255537 🚋 Tram 4, 9, 14, 16, 24, 25

ANALIK

Simple, elegant designs are the hallmark of this boutique belonging to Anakujm, considered Amsterdam's foremost young designer.

✚ E4 ✉ Hartenstraat 36 ☎ 4220561 🚋 Tram 1, 2, 5, 13, 14, 17

ANIMATION ART

Pictures and figurines of famous cartoon characters from Superman to Tintin and the Smurfs.

✚ F4 ✉ Gravenstracht 8 ☎ 6222203 🚋 Tram 1, 2, 4, 5, 9, 13, 16, 17, 24, 25

ATHENAEUM BOEKHANDEL

This bookshop, in a striking art nouveau building, specializes in social sciences, literature and the classics, and stocks international newspapers.

✚ E5 ✉ Spui 14–16 ☎ 6226248 🚋 Tram 1, 2, 5

DE BIERKONING

Beers and glasses from around the world.

✚ E5 ✉ Paleisstraat 125 ☎ 6252336 🚋 Tram 1, 2, 5, 13, 14, 17

DE BIJENKORF

Amsterdam's busy main department store, the *Bijenkorf* (Beehive) lives up to its name.

✚ F4 ✉ Dam 1 ☎ 0900 0919 (premium rate) 🚋 Tram 4, 9, 14, 16, 24, 25

BONEBAKKER

www.bonebakker.nl
Holland's royal jewellers, with dazzling displays of gold and silverware. Enjoyable even if you can't afford to buy.

✚ F5 ✉ Rokin 88–90 ☎ 6232294 🚋 Tram 4, 9, 14, 16, 24, 25

MAGNA PLAZA

Amsterdam's most luxurious shopping mall, Magna Plaza, is in an imposing neo-Gothic building, which was formerly the city's main post office, in Nieuwzijds Voorburgwal near the Dam. Its four floors are filled with upscale specialist shops, such as Pinokkio, for educational toys; Bjorn Borg, for sporty underwear; and Speeldozenwereld, for quaint musical boxes. There is a café on the top floor.

CONDOMERIE

www.condomerie.com
The world's first specialist condom shop—fun but with a serious approach to sexual hygenie and safe sex.

✚ F4 ✉ Warmoesstraat 141 ☎ 6274174 🚋 Tram 4, 9, 14, 16, 24, 25

DAM SQUARE SOUVENIRS

www.damsquare.com
This souvenir shop has a choice of clogs, furnishings, wooden tulips, windmills, Delft pottery, miniature bicycles and T-shirts.

✚ F4 ✉ Dam 17 ☎ 6203432 🚋 Tram 4, 9, 14, 16, 24, 25

DEN HAAN & WAGENMAKERS

A quilt-maker's paradise of traditional fabrics, tools and gadgets. Closed Sunday to Wednesday.

✚ F4 ✉ Nieuwezijds Voorburgwal 97–99 ☎ 6202525 🚋 Tram 1, 2, 5, 13, 17

EGIDIUS ANTIQUARISCHE BOEKHANDEL

A tiny shop packed to the gunnels with antique books on travel, photography and the arts.

✚ E5 ✉ Nieuwezijds Voorburgwal 334 ☎ 6243929 🚋 Tram 1, 2, 5

ESPRIT

Young, trendy designs for the seriously fashionable.

✚ E5 ✉ Spui 10a ☎ 6263624 🚋 Tram 1, 2, 5

GASTRONOMIE NOSTALGIE

www.gastronomienostalgie.nl
Specializes in antique silver, silver-plated objects, porcelain, glass and crystal. This is the sort of tableware that was used in the heyday of hotels such as the Ritz, the Carlton and the Hotel de Paris.

🔢 E5 ✉ Nieuwezijds Voorburgwal 304 ☎ 4226226 🚋 Tram 1, 2, 5

GEELS EN CO

Holland's oldest coffee-roasting and tea-trading company, full of heady aromas, with a helpful staff and traditional setting.

🔢 F4 ✉ Warmoesstraat 67 ☎ 6240683 🚋 Tram 4, 9, 14, 16, 24, 25

HEAD SHOP

The shop for marijuana paraphernalia and memorabilia ever since it opened in the 1960s.

🔢 G5 ✉ Kloveniersburgwal 39 ☎ 6249061 Ⓜ Nieuwmarkt

HEMP WORKS

Designer hemp shop: jeans, jackets, shirts, shampoo and soap all made of hemp.

🔢 F4 ✉ Nieuwendijk 13 ☎ 4211762 🚋 Tram 1, 2, 5, 13, 17

HESTER VAN EEGHEN

Handbags, wallets and other leather accessories in innovative shapes, styles and hues, designed in Holland and made in Italy.

🔢 E4 ✉ Hartenstraat 37 ☎ 6269212 🚋 Tram 13, 14, 17

HOLLAND GALLERY DE MUNT

Miniature ceramic canal houses, dolls in traditional costume, ornately decorated wooden boxes and trays. Also antique Delftware, royal and Makkumer pottery and traditional tiles.

🔢 F6 ✉ Muntplein 12 ☎ 6232271 🚋 Tram 4, 9, 14, 16, 24, 25

H. P. DE VRENG

Celebrated wine-and-spirits establishment, producing fine liqueurs and *jenevers* since 1852.

🔢 F4 ✉ Nieuwendijk 75 ☎ 6244581 🚋 Tram 1, 2, 5, 6, 13, 17

MORE TIPS

Most shops are open Tuesday to Saturday from 9am or 10am until 6pm, on Monday from 1pm until 6pm, on Thursday until 9pm. Many shops open 12–5pm on Sunday, too. Cash is the usual method of payment, although credit cards are accepted at most department stores and most of the larger shops.

If you want to browse in the smaller shops it is customary practice to greet the owner who will be only too happy for you to look.

JACOB HOOIJ

Old-fashioned apothecary, selling herbs, spices and homeopathic remedies since 1743. All earthenware jars and 19th-century drawers full of aromatherapy remedies and health foods.

🔢 G5 ✉ Kloveniersburgwal 12 ☎ 6243041 Ⓜ Nieuwmarkt

MAISON DE BONNETERIE

www.debonneterie.nl
A gracious department store, popular with wealthy ladies.

🔢 F5 ✉ Rokin 140–142/ Kalverstraat 183 ☎ 5313400 🚋 Tram 4, 9, 14, 16, 24, 25

METZ & CO

Expensive gifts and designer funiture in one of the city's most stylish department stores. It has a café on the top floor.

🔢 F6 ✉ Keizersgracht 455 ☎ 5207020 🚋 Tram 1, 2, 5

NIC NIC

Irresistible knickknacks shop selling 1950s to 1970s collectibles and near-antiques, all in good condition.

🔢 E5 ✉ Gasthuismolensteeg 5 ☎ 6228523 🚋 Tram 1, 2, 5

OILILY

www.oilily-world.com
Located in the Kalvertoren shopping mall, this Dutch chain store, with shops globally, specializes in bright and cheerful clothing for kids and their mums.

F6 ✉ Singel 457,
Kalvertoren ☎ 4228713
🚊 Tram 1, 4, 9, 14, 16, 24, 25

OSCAR

Outrageous footwear,
from glittery platforms to
psychedelic thigh boots.
F4 ✉ Nieuwendijk
208–10 ☎ 6253143
🚊 Tram 4, 9, 14, 16, 24, 25

PALETTE

What's said to be the
smallest shop in the
Netherlands has a large
selection of silk and satin
shoes, in 500 shades.
F4 ✉ Nieuwezijds
Voorburgwal 125 ☎ 6393207
🚊 Tram 4, 9, 14, 16, 24, 25

PAARS LINGERIE

www.parslingerie.com
The most extensive collection of lingerie in the
Netherlands. This large
luxurious store sells all the
top international brands.
E5 ✉ Spuistraat 242
☎ 6182828 🚊 Tram 1, 2, 5

P. G. C. HAJENIUS

www.hajenius.com
One of the world's finest
tobacco shops, in elegant,
art deco premises; in business for more than 250
years.
F5 ✉ Rokin 92–96
☎ 6237494 🚊 Tram 4, 9,
14, 16, 24, 25

SCHELTEMA, HOLKEMA EN VERMEULEN

The city's biggest book-
shop, with a floor of com-
puter software and audio
and video titles.

E6 ✉ Koningsplein 20
☎ 5231411 🚊 Tram 1, 2, 5

DE SLEGTE

www.desleghte.nl
Amsterdam's largest
second-hand bookshop is
good for bargains.
F5 ✉ Kalverstraat 48–52
☎ 6225933 🚊 Tram 4, 9,
14, 16, 24, 25

VITALS VITAMIN-ADVICE SHOP

www.vitaminadviceshop.nl
Vitamins and other food
supplements, plus a
unique service: A compu-
terized test that proposes
vitamin supplements
based on age and lifestyle.
F4 ✉ Nieuwe
Nieuwstraat 47 ☎ 4274747
🚊 Tram 1, 2, 5, 6, 13, 17

VROOM & DREESMANN

www.vroomendressmann.nl
Clothing, jewellery, per-
fumes, electronics, leather
goods, watches, clothing

for all the family and
household goods. V&D
has good quality at rea-
sonable prices.
F5 ✉ Kalverstraat
201–203 ☎ 0900 2358363
(premium rate) 🚊 Tram 4, 9,
14, 16, 20, 24, 25

WATERSTONE'S

Reliable English-language
bookshop plus English
newspapers and
magazines and good
guidebooks selection.
F5 ✉ Kalverstraat 152
☎ 6383821 🚊 1, 2, 4, 5, 9,
14, 16, 24, 25

WEBER'S HOLLAND

Fantastical and occasion-
ally straight-out bizarre
clothing and accessories,
in the historic setting of
the Klein Trippenhuis.
G5 ✉ Kloveniersburgwal
26 ☎ 6381777
🚇 Nieuwmarkt

WONDERWOOD

www.wonderwood.nl
A combination of shop
and gallery, Wonderwood
is all about vintage ply-
wood design from the
1940s to 1960s. The
shop features more than
100 vintage plywood
design chairs and re-
editions are for sale.
F5 ✉ Rusland 3
☎ 6253738 🚊 Tram 4, 9, 14

WOUT ARXHOEK

One of the best cheese
shops, with more than
250 different varieties.
F4 ✉ Damstraat 19
☎ 6229118 🚊 Tram 4, 9, 14,
16, 20, 24, 25

Entertainment and Nightlife

AKHNATON

Funky multicultural youth venue with reggae, rap and salsa dance nights. Be prepared for close dancing—this place gets full.

➕ F4 ✉ Nieuwezijds Kolk 25 ☎ 6243396 🚋 Tram 1, 2, 5, 6, 13, 17

AMSTERDAM MARIONETTE THEATRE

www.marionet.demon.nl
Traditional puppet shows can be seen in this former blacksmith's. Opera is its specialty.

➕ G4 ✉ Nieuwe Jonkerstraat 8 ☎ 6208027 🚋 Tram 1, 2, 5, 6, 13, 17

ARC

www.bararc.com
Great atmosphere at this recently opened classy cocktail bar and restaurant for straight and gay alike. Open every day from 10am, there is music and dancing until the early hours.

➕ F6 ✉ Reguliersdwarsstraat 44 ☎ 6897070 🚋 Tram 1, 2, 5

DE BEIAARD

www.beiaardgroup.nl
A beer drinker's paradise—over 80 beers from around the world.

➕ E5 ✉ Spui 30 ☎ 6225110 🚋 Tram 1, 2, 5

BEURS VAN BERLAGE

Home to the Netherlands Philharmonic Orchestra and Dutch Chamber Orchestra, this remarkable early modernist building that once housed the stock exchange makes an impressive concert hall.

➕ F4 ✉ Damrak 213 ☎ 6270466 🚋 Tram 4, 9, 16, 24, 25

CAFÉ APRIL

www.reguliersdwars.nl/april
Popular, easy-going gay bar that attracts a mixed crowd of mostly male locals and tourists.

➕ F6 ✉ Reguliersdwarsstraat 37 ☎ 6259572 🚋 Tram 1, 2, 5

CAFÉ DANTE

www.dante.nl
A good choice if you want to be with the young, good-looking crowd.

➕ E5 ✉ Spuistraat 320 ☎ 638839 🚋 Tram 1, 2, 5

BAR TALK

Most of the 1,402 bars and cafés in Amsterdam are open from around 10am until the early hours and many serve meals. *Proeflokalen* open from around 4pm until 8pm, and some serve snacks, such as nuts, cheese, meatballs and sausage. Beer is the most popular alcoholic drink. It is always served with a head, and often with a *jenever* chaser called a *kopstoot* (a blow to the head). If you want only a small beer, ask for a *colatje* or *kleintjepils*. Belgian beers are increasingly popular in Holland, and are considered more of a craft product.

DANSEN BIJ JANSEN

www.dansenbijjansen.nl
Student disco playing the latest chart toppers. You need student ID or be with a student, to get in.

➕ E3 ✉ Handboogstraat 11 ☎ 6201779 🕐 Daily 11pm–4am 🚋 Tram 1, 2, 5

DE DRIE FLESCHJES

Amsterdammers have been tasting gins at the Three Little Bottles since 1650.

➕ F4 ✉ Gravenstraat 18 ☎ 6248443 🚋 Tram 1, 2, 4, 5, 6, 9, 13, 14, 16, 17, 24, 25

DE DUIVEL

Amsterdam's only hip-hop club that opened in 1992 and staying close to its roots with rap and hip-hop beats and a crowd to match. Occasional live music at the weekends until 3am.

➕ F6 ✉ Reguliersdwarsstraat 87 ☎ 6266184 🚋 Tram 1, 2, 5

DE ENGELBE-WAARDER

Jazz on Sunday from 4pm livens up a usually tranquil, arty hangout just off the Red Light District.

➕ F5 ✉ Kloveniersburgwal 59 ☎ 6253772 🚇 Nieuwmarkt

ENGELSE KERK

A chance to hear some excellent weekly baroque and choral concerts in tranquil surroundings.

➕ E5 ✉ Begijnhof 48 ☎ 6249665 🚋 Tram 1, 2, 4, 5, 9, 14, 16, 24, 25

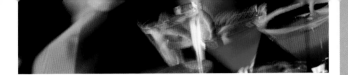

DE HEEREN VAN AEMSTEL

www.deheerenvanaemstel.nl
Prior to events such as The Hagues' North Sea Jazz Festival, you can often see some of the world's great jazz performers here.
➕ F6 ✉ Thorbeckeplein 5
☎ 6202173 🚊 Tram 4, 9, 14

HOPPE

One of Amsterdam's most established, most popular brown cafés, with beer in one bar and gin from the barrel in another.
➕ E5 ✉ Spui 18–20
☎ 4204420 🚊 Tram 1, 2, 5

JANSEN AEROBIC FITNESSCENTRUM

Fitness venue with gyms, sauna, solarium and daily aerobics classes.
➕ F5 ✉ Rokin 109–111
☎ 6269366 🚊 Tram 4, 9, 14, 16, 24, 25

DE JAREN

A spacious, ultramodern café, known for its trendy clientele. Sunny terraces overlooking the Amstel.
➕ F5 ✉ Nieuwe Doelenstraat 20–22
☎ 6255771 🚊 Tram 4, 9, 14, 16, 24, 25

MINISTRY

A classy café-cum-nightclub with all kinds of disco music. Intimate atmosphere.
➕ F6 ✉ Reguliersdwarsstraat
☎ 6233981 🕐 Wed–Sun 11pm–4/5am 🚊 Tram 1, 2, 4, 5, 9, 14, 16, 24, 25

NIEUWE KERK

www.nieuwekerk.nl
Frequent lunchtime concerts and exceptional organ recitals by visiting organists, in an atmospheric setting (▷ 47).
➕ F4 ✉ Dam ☎ 6268168
🚊 Tram 1, 2, 4, 5, 9, 13, 14, 16, 17, 24, 25

ODEON

www.odeontheater.nl
A converted canal house with house music on the first floor, 1960s–'80s classic disco upstairs and jazz in the basement.
➕ F6 ✉ Singel 460
☎ 6249711 🕐 Thu–Sat 11–4am, Fri, Sat until 5am
🚊 Tram 1, 2, 5

DE OOIEVAAR

A homey atmosphere pervades The Stork, one of Holland's smallest proeflokalen.
➕ G4 ✉ Sint-Olofspoort 1

'DUTCH COURAGE'

Dutch gin (jenever), made from molasses and laced with juniper berries, comes in a variety of ages: jong (young), oud (old) and zeer oud (the oldest and the mellowest), and in shades ranging from clear to brownish. Other interesting tastes may be added; try bessenjenever (blackcurrant), or bitterkoekjes likeur (macaroon).
Jenever is drunk straight or as a beer chaser, not with a mixer. Dutch for cheers is Proost!

☎ 4208004 🚇 Centraal Station

O'REILLY'S IRISH PUB

www.oreillys.com
Choice whiskeys and hearty Irish fare accompanied by jolly folk music with a warm and friendly welcome.
➕ E5 ✉ Paleisstraat 103–105
☎ 6249498 🚊 Tram 1, 2, 5

OUDE KERK

www.oudekerk.nl
Chamber music concerts and organ recitals are held in this old church, where Holland's foremost composer, Jan Pieters zoon Sweelinck (1562–1621) was once organist. Pass by at 4pm on Saturday, and you may hear a carillon concert (▷ 48).
➕ G4 ✉ Oudekerksplein 23
☎ 6258284 🚇 Nieuwmark
🚊 Tram 4, 9, 6, 24, 251

SUPPERCLUB

www.supperclub.nl
This is an Amsterdam legend and much more than a dining experience. White mattresses, silver plates, plenty of music, live cabaret and complete relaxation. You eat off your lap while reclining and can also take a massage between courses. Set aside four hours for the dinner. Just be aware that anything goes here and it is not for the sensitive or prudish.
➕ E5 ✉ Jonge Roelenssteeg 21 ☎ 3446400 🚊 Tram 1, 2, 4, 13, 14, 16, 17, 24, 25

TUCHINSKI THEATER
Holland's most attractive and prestigious cinema, with six screens. The classic art deco interior, complete with eight-person boxes and champagne, alone makes it worth visiting, no matter what's showing.
🔒 F6 ☒ Reguliersbreestraat 26–34 ☎ 4281060 🚋 Tram 4, 9, 14, 20

WINSTON KINGDOM
www.winston.nl
Loud, live rock music is the attraction most nights at this club, bar and restaurant in the Red Light District.
🔒 F4 ☒ Warmoesstraat 131 ☎ 6231380 🚋 Tram 4, 9, 16

WYNAND FOCKINK
www.wynardfockink.nl
Hidden down a side alley off the Dam, this charming 1679 *proeflokaal* serves 100 or so gins and liquers, some made at the next-door Janssens distillery. If the weather is warm, seek out the charming courtyard garden but note, mobile phones are banned.
🔒 F4 ☒ Pijlsteeg 31 ☎ 6392695 🚋 Tram 4, 9, 14, 16, 24, 25

Restaurants

PRICES
Prices are approximate, based on a 3-course meal for one person.
€€€ over €40
€€ €20–€40
€ under €20

1E KLAS (€)
This café (pronounced 'Eerste Klas') is on Platform Two in the old first-class waiting rooms at Amsterdam's Centraal Station. Enjoy delicious coffee and cakes in the grand old style of steam travel.
🔒 G3 ☒ Centraal Station, Stationsplein 15 ☎ 6250131 🕐 Daily 9am–11pm 🚉 Centraal Station 🚋 Tram 1, 2, 4, 5, 6, 9, 13, 16, 17, 24, 25

ANEKA RASA (€€)
This airy modern restaurant offers numerous vegetarian dishes including an all-vegetarian *rijsttafel*. Attentive friendly staff serve amid a tropical ambience.
🔒 G4 ☒ Warmoesstraat 25–29, Centrum ☎ 6261560 🕐 Dinner only 🚉 Centraal Station

COFFEE SHOPS
In Amsterdam, the expression 'coffee shop' refers to the 'smoking' coffee shops, where mostly young people hang out, high on hash. 'Smoking' coffee shops are usually easily recognizable by their psychedelic decor, thick fog of bitter smoke and mellow clientele. The cake on sale is sure to be drug-laced 'space cake'. Surprisingly, many such shops do a good cup of coffee. For just coffee you need to look out for a straightforward café or *kaffehuis*.

DE BRAKKE GROND (€–€€)
www.brasseriedebrakkegrond.nl
The Flemish Cultural Centre's darkly atmospheric restaurant with a spacious terrace, serving bountiful portions of Belgian food. There is a great choice of Belgian beers to complement your meal.
🔒 F5 ☒ Nes 43, Centrum ☎ 6260044 🕐 Mon–Thu 11am–1am, Fri, Sat 11am–2am, Sun noon–1am 🚋 Tram 4, 9, 14, 16, 24, 25

CAFÉ PACIFICO (€)
www.cafepacifico.nl
The most authentic Mexican *bodega* in town. It gets especially crowded on Tuesday, which is margarita night when everyone is partying.
🔒 G4 ☒ Warmoesstraat 31, Centrum ☎ 6242911 🕐 Daily lunch, dinner 🚉 Centraal Station

CAFÉ ROUX (€€)
www.thegrand.nl
Fine French cuisine in an art nouveau setting, overlooked by a Karel Appel mural.
🕂 F4 ✉ Grand Hotel, Oudezijds Voorburgwal 197, Centrum ☎ 5553560 🕓 Daily lunch, dinner 🚇 Nieuwmarkt 🚋 Tram 4, 9, 14, 16, 24, 25

CAFFÉ ESPRIT (€)
Designer café, all glass and aluminium, run by the clothing chain next door. Sandwiches, salads, burgers and bagels. You can sit outside when the weather is fine.
🕂 E5 ✉ Spui 10a, Centrum ☎ 6221967 🕓 Mon–Sat 10–6 (also Thu until 10pm), Sun noon–6 🚋 Tram 1, 2, 4, 5, 9, 14, 16, 24, 25

CHEZ GEORGES (€€)
Fine Belgian cuisine in a candlelight setting.
🕂 E4 ✉ Herenstraat 3, Grachtengordel ☎ 6263332 🕓 Dinner only, closed Sun, Wed 🚋 Tram 1, 2, 5, 13, 17

DORRIUS (€€€)
A sophisticated take on the rustic Dutch style. Sample the pike and cod traditional delicacies, or the cheese soufflé.
🕂 F4 ✉ Crowne Plaza Hotel, Nieuwezijds Voorburgwal 5, Centrum ☎ 4202224 🕓 Tue–Sat 6pm–11pm 🚋 Tram 1, 2, 5, 13, 17

DYNASTY (€€€)
A sophisticated, sumptuously decorated garden restaurant with fine Southeast Asian cuisine.
🕂 F6 ✉ Reguliersdwarsstraat 30, Grachtengordel ☎ 6268400 🕓 Wed–Mon dinner only 🚋 Tram 16, 24, 25

FROMAGERIE CRIGNON CULINAIR (€)
Rustic restaurant with eight different types of cheese fondue.
🕂 F4 ✉ Gravenstraat 28, Centrum ☎ 6246428 🕓 Tue–Sun dinner only 🚋 Tram 4, 9, 14, 16, 24, 25

GREENWOOD'S (€)
Homey little English-style tearoom serving up scones with jam and cream, chocolate cake and lemon-meringue pie. You can sit outside in summer.
🕂 F4 ✉ Singel 103, Grachtengordel ☎ 6237071 🕓 Daily 9.30–7 🚋 Tram 1, 2, 5, 6, 13, 17

TIPPING

Most restaurant windows display menus giving the price of individual dishes including BTW (value-added tax) and a 15 per cent service charge. You don't really need to worry too much about tipping but nevertheless, most Amsterdammers leave a small tip or round up the bill (check). This tip should be left as change rather than included on a credit-card payment. If you feel you have good service then that's the time to leave a tip.

HAESJE CLAES (€€)
www.haesjeclaes.nl
Dutch cuisine at its best, served in a warren of small, panelled dining rooms in a building dating from the 16th-century.
🕂 E5 ✉ Spuistraat 275, Centrum ☎ 6249998 🕓 Daily lunch, dinner 🚋 Tram 1, 2, 5

HET KARBEEL (€–€€)
www.hetkarbeel.nl
A café/restaurant serving everything from hearty breakfasts and light lunches to filling full meals in pleasant surroundings. You can sit up in the gallery.
🕂 G4 ✉ Warmoesstraat 16, Centrum ☎ 6274995 🕓 Daily 9.30am–11pm 🚇 Centraal Station

KANTJIL & DE TIJGER (€€)
Modern decor and spicy, imaginative Javanese cuisine. Try the delicious *Nasi Rames*, a mini-*rijsttafel* on one plate.
🕂 E5 ✉ Spuistraat 291, Centrum ☎ 6200994 🕓 Dinner only 🚋 Tram 1, 2, 5

KEUKEN VAN 1870 (€)
www.keukenvan1870.nl
This onetime soup kitchen, renovated and a shade gentrified, serves up wholesome and hearty Dutch fare for a modest price.
🕂 F3 ✉ Spuistraat 4, Centrum ☎ 6204018 🕓 Dinner only 🚋 Tram 1, 2, 5, 13, 17

MEMORIES OF INDIA (€€€)

www.memoriesofindia.nl
Tandoori, Moghlai and vegetarian cuisine in a refined colonial setting.

🔳 F6 ✉ Reguliersdwarsstraat 88, Grachtengordel
☎ 6235710 🕙 Dinner only
🚊 Tram 4, 9, 14, 16, 24, 25

MORITA-YA (€)

www.morita-ya.orientalrestaurants.nl
Traditional Japanese snackbar that's a must for sushi fans.

🔳 G4 ✉ Zeedijk 18, Centrum ☎ 6380756
🕙 Tue–Sun dinner only
🚊 Centraal Station

NIEUWE KAFÉ (€)

www.nieuwekafe.nl
The café's crowded terrace on the Dam provides a captive audience for street musicians; ideal for people-watching.

🔳 F4 ✉ Eggertstraat 8, Centrum ☎ 6272830
🕙 Daily 9–6 🚊 Tram 4, 9, 14, 16, 24, 25

OCHO LATIN GRILL (€€–€€€)

www.ochogrill.nl
Stylish restaurant offering some of the best grilled food in town. High-quality beef raised on the South American pampas is a popular choice. If red meat is not for you, try the excellent chicken, fish, salads and fajitas.

🔳 F6 ✉ Reguliersdwarsstraat 8, Grachtengordel
☎ 6250592 🕙 Daily 5pm–11pm 🚊 Tram 1, 2, 5

LE PECHEUR (€€€)

A smart fish-bistro with a secluded garden. Outstanding fresh oysters, caviar, sashimi and succulent lobster.

🔳 F6 ✉ Reguliersdwarsstraat 32, Grachtengordel
☎ 6243121 🕙 Closed Sat lunch and all day Sun
🚊 Tram 1, 2, 5

LA PLACE (€)

A self-service 'indoor market' restaurant can be found inside the department store Vroom & Dreesmann (▷ 57). There is a great choice at reasonable prices. Choose your dish at one of the stands, watch it being cooked, then eat at the tables. Terrific juices.

🔳 F5 ✉ Rokin 164, Centrum
☎ 0900 2358365 (premium rate) 🕙 Daily 10–8 (Thu 10.30–9, Sun–Mon 11–8)
🚊 Tram 4, 9, 14, 16, 24, 25

A HEARTY MEAL

When the Dutch took over the Spice Islands of the East Indies in the 17th century, they got more than spices out of their new colony. They developed a taste for the exotic local cuisine that survived Indonesian independence and gives Amsterdam today an abundance of *Indonesisch* restaurants. First-timers to an Indonesian restaurant should order a *rijsttafel*–rice and a complete range of other meat, fish, egg and vegetable dishes.

DE POORT (€€)

Since 1870, this famous restaurant has sold more than 6 million numbered steaks. Every thousandth lucky diner gets a free bottle of house wine.

🔳 F4 ✉ Hotel Die Port van Cleve, Nieuwezijds Voorburgwal 176, Centrum
☎ 6240047 🕙 Daily lunch, dinner 🚊 Tram 1, 2, 5, 13, 17

EL RANCHO ARGENTINIAN (€€)

Sizzling steaks and spare ribs in a wood-panelled, jolly-gaucho setting that brings a taste of the South American pampas to Amsterdam.

🔳 E5 ✉ Spui 3, Centrum
☎ 6256764 🕙 Daily 11am–midnight 🚊 Tram 4, 9, 14, 16, 24

DE ROODE LEEUW (€€)

The brasserie-style Red Lion serves up good stews and sauerkraut dishes.

🔳 F4 ✉ Hotel Amsterdam, Damrak 93–94, Centrum
☎ 5550666 🕙 Daily 7am–11pm, last orders 9.30pm
🚊 Tram 4, 9, 14, 16, 24, 25

ROSE'S CANTINA (€€)

www.rosescantina.com
Excellent value Tex-Mex meals in lively, sociable surroundings. This is probably Amsterdam's most crowded and popular restaurant.

🔳 F6 ✉ Reguliersdwarsstraat 38-40, Grachtengordel
☎ 6259797 🕙 Dinner only from 5pm 🚊 Tram 4, 9, 14, 16, 24, 25

3

4

5

6

7

E

F

G

Scheepvaarthuis

Lastageweg

Oude

Recht Boomssloot

Recht Boomssloot

Koningsstraat

Keizersstr

St Antoniesbreestr

Nwe Hoogstr

Krom Boomssl

Oudeschans

Oudeschans

Dijkstr

Zandstr

Raamgr

Raamgr

Zuiderkerk

Museum Het Rembrandthuis

Groenburgwal

Groenburgwal

Zwanenburgwal

Jodenbreestr

Waterlooplein

Stadhuis

Waterlooplein

Waterlooplein Flea Market

M Visserplein

Groenburgwal

Amstel

Stopera

Muziek-theater

AMSTEL

WATERLOOPLEIN

Joods Historisch Museum

Nieuwe

Rembrandt-plein

Paarden-str

Wagen-str

Amstelstr

Hermitage Amsterdam

Amstelhof

Nieuwe

Nieuw

Museum Willet Holthuysen

Herengracht

Herengracht

Thorbecke-plein

Herengracht

Herengracht

Six Collection

Amstel

Amstel

VIZELSTRAAT

Herengracht

Keizersgracht

Museum Fodor

Utrechtsestraat

Keizersgracht

Keizersgracht

Nwe Spiegelstraat

Keizersgracht

Reguliersgracht

Kerkstraat

Magere Brug

Museum Van Loon

Bur Civitas

Kerkstraat

Theater Carré

Kerkstraat

Reguliers-gracht

Reguliers-gracht

Prinsengracht

Prinsengracht

Amstel-sluizen

Spiegel-gracht

1e Wetering dw- str

Wetering-str

2e Wetering dw- str

Prinsengracht

Amstelkerk

Prinsengracht

Utrechtsedwarsstraat

Achter-gracht

3e Wetering dw- str

Noorderstr

Reguliers-gracht

VIZELGRACHT

Lijnbaansgracht

Nwe Looiersstr

Falck-str

Frederiks-plein

M J Kosterstr

F. Simonszstraat

Lijnbaansgracht

Joods Historisch Museum

Silver Hanukkah lamp (left) on display at the Jewish Historical Museum (right)

A remarkable exhibition devoted to Judaism and the story of Jewish settlement in Amsterdam. The most memorable and poignant part portrays the horrors of the Holocaust.

THE BASICS

www.jhm.nl
🔲 G6
✉ Jonas Daniël Meijerplein 2–4
☎ 5310310
🕐 Daily 11–5. Closed Yom Kippur
🍴 Café 🚇 Waterlooplein
🚊 Tram 9, 14,
🚢 Museumboat stop 3
♿ Very good
💰 Expensive

HIGHLIGHTS

● Grote Schul (Great Synagogue, 1671)
● Holy Ark (1791)
● Haggadah Manuscript (1734)

DID YOU KNOW?

● 1597—The first Jew gained Dutch citizenship.
● 1602—Judaism was first practised openly here.
● 102,000 of the 140,000-strong Dutch Jewish community were exterminated in World War II.

Reconstruction In the heart of what used to be a Jewish neighbourhood, this massive complex of four former synagogues forms the largest and most important Jewish museum outside Israel. The buildings lay in ruins for many years after World War II, but have since been reconstructed, at a cost of €6 million, as a monument to the strength of the Jewish faith and to the suffering of the Jewish people under the Nazis.

Historical exhibits The New Synagogue (1752) gives a lengthy, detailed history of Zionism, with displays of religious objects. The Great Synagogue (1671), of more general interest, defines the role of the Jewish community in Amsterdam's trade and industry. Downstairs is a chilling exhibition from the war years and a moving collection by Jewish painters.

The Dockworker The Nazis occupied Amsterdam in May 1940 and immediately began to persecute the Jewish population. In February 1941, 400 Jews were gathered outside the Great Synagogue by the SS, herded into trucks and taken away. This triggered the February Strike, a general strike led by dockers. Though suppressed after only two days, it was Amsterdam's first open revolt against Nazism and gave impetus to the resistance movement.

The Magere Brug or Skinny Bridge looks attractive illuminated at night

Magere Brug

This traditional double-leaf Dutch drawbridge is a city landmark, and one of the most photographed sights in Amsterdam at night, illuminated by strings of enchanting lights.

Skinny sisters Of Amsterdam's 1,200 or so bridges, the wooden 'Skinny Bridge' is, without doubt, the best known. On the Amstel river, it is a 20th-century replica of a 17th-century drawbridge. Tradition has it that, in 1670, a simple footbridge was built by two elderly sisters named Mager (meaning skinny), who lived on one side of the Amstel and wanted easy access to their carriage and horses, stabled on the other bank. It seems more likely, however, that the bridge took its name from its narrow girth. In 1772 it was widened and became a double drawbridge, enabling ships of heavy tonnage to sail up the Amstel from the IJ, an inlet of what was then a sea called the Zuider Zee and is today the IJsselmeer, a freshwater lake.

City uproar In 1929 the city council started discussing whether to demolish the old frame, which had rotted. It was to be replaced with an electrically operated bridge. After a huge outcry, the people of Amsterdam voted overwhelmingly to save the original wooden bridge.

Latest crossing The present bridge, made of African azobe wood, was erected in 1969 and its mechanical drive installed in 1994. Its graceful proportions are still pleasing to the eye.

THE BASICS

- ✚ G6
- ✉ At Kerkstraat on the Amstel river
- Ⓦ Waterlooplein
- 🚃 Tram 4
- 🚤 Museumboat stop 3

DID YOU KNOW?

- Around 63,000 boats pass under the bridge each year.
- The rebuilding of the bridge in 1969 cost €63,530.
- There are 60 drawbridges in Amsterdam; 8 are wooden.

Museum Het Rembrandthuis

TOP 25

Not always respected during his lifetime, Rembrandt's image and work is everywhere

THE BASICS

www.rembrandthuis.nl
➕ G5
✉ Jodenbreestraat 4
☎ 5200400
🕐 Daily 10–5 (until 9pm on Fri). Closed 1 Jan, and some short periods during the year, call to confirm
Ⓜ Nieuwmarkt, Waterlooplein
🚊 Tram 9, 14
⛴ Museumboat stop 3
♿ Few
💷 Expensive
❓ Brief film of Rembrandt's life

HIGHLIGHTS

- *Self-portrait with a Surprised Expression*
- *Five Studies of the Head of Saskia and one of an Older Woman*
- *View of Amsterdam*
- *Christ Shown to the People*

The absence of Rembrandt's own belongings from this intimate house is more than compensated for by its collection of his etchings, which is virtually complete. They are fascinating.

From riches to rags In this red-shuttered canal house, Rembrandt spent the happiest and most successful years of his life, producing many of his most famous paintings and prints here. Through his wife, the wealthy heiress Saskia van Uylenburg, the up-and-coming young artist had been introduced to Amsterdam's patrician class and commissions for portraits had poured in. He had rapidly become an esteemed painter, and bought this large, three-storey house in 1639 as a symbol of his newfound respectability. After Saskia's tragic death, age 30, in 1642 shortly after the birth of their son Titus, Rembrandt's work became unfashionable, and in 1656 he was declared bankrupt. The house and most of his possessions were sold in 1658, although Rembrandt continued to live here until 1660. He died a pauper in 1669.

Funny faces Rembrandt's achievements in etching (many created in this house) were as important as those in his painting, since his mastery in this medium inspired its recognition as an art form for the first time. Four of his copper etching plates are also on display, together with a series of biblical illustrations. Look out for Rembrandt's studies of street figures hung alongside some highly entertaining self-portraits in various guises, and some mirror-images of himself making faces.

Both inside and out, the Willet-Holthuysen museum oozes classical elegance

Museum Willet-Holthuysen

Behind the impressive façade of this beautifully preserved, gracious mansion lies a lavishly decorated, sumptuously furnished home with a delightful garden, a rare luxury in Amsterdam.

Insight Standing on Herengracht, Amsterdam's most elegant canal (▷ 44), this house was built in 1687 for Jacob Hop, a wealthy member of the city council. It changed hands many times and eventually, in 1855, came into the possession of a glass merchant named Pieter Gerard Holthuysen. On his death, it became the home of his daughter Sandra and her husband, the art collector Abraham Willet, who together built up a valuable collection of glass, silver, ceramics and paintings. The couple bequeathed the house and its contents to the city in 1895, to be used as a museum. For many years it was visited rarely. However, following extensive restoration in the late 1990s, the museum attracts an increasing number of visitors, and provides a rare insight into life in the grand canal-houses in the 17th to 19th centuries.

Luxury and grandeur The rooms are decorated with inlaid wood and lacquered panelling with painted ceilings. Be sure to see the Blue Room, formerly the preserve of the gentlemen of the house, and the 17th-century kitchen, with its original plumbing. Guests would be served tea in the tiny, round Garden Room that, painted in the customary pale green, looks out over an immaculate French-style formal garden This rare 18th-century garden is a jewel not to be missed.

THE BASICS

www.willetholthuysen.nl
✚ G6
✉ Herengracht 605
☎ 5231822
🕐 Mon–Fri 10–5, Sat–Sun and public hols 11–5. Closed 1 Jan, 30 Apr, 25 Dec
🚇 Waterlooplein
🚊 Tram 4, 9, 14
🚢 Museumboat stop 3
♿ None
💶 Moderate

HIGHLIGHTS

- Blue Room
- Dining Room
- Porcelain and silver collections
- Kitchen
- Garden Room
- Garden

Nederlands Scheepvaart Museum

HIGHLIGHTS

● The *Amsterdam*
● Royal sloop
● Blaeu's World Atlas
● First printed map of
Amsterdam
● Three-masted ship
● Wartime exhibits

TIPS

● Check in advance if there
are any special activities
planned.
● Mind your head as you go
around the ship unless you
are below 1m (3ft 4in) tall.

Holland's glorious seafaring history gets due recognition at this museum, which displays with contemporary flair a fine collection of ships, full-size replicas, and models and artefacts.

Admiralty storehouse The vast neoclassical building (1656) that now houses the Maritime Museum was formerly the Dutch Admiralty's central store. Here the United East India Company (VOC) would load their ships prior to the eight-month journey to Jakarta, headquarters of the VOC in Indonesia. In 1973, the arsenal was converted into this museum, which has the largest collection of ships in the world.

Voyages of discovery An ancient dugout, a re-created section of a destroyer, luxury liners and

The delightful and superbly decorated stern of the replica of the Amsterdam, *an 18th-century Dutch East Indiaman (left)*
Amsterdam's Maritime Museum's most popular exhibit is moored alongside the building that houses a fascinating seafaring collection

schooners depict Holland's remarkable maritime history. Peer through periscopes and operate a radar set, marvel at some 500 magnificent model ships and study the charts, instruments, weapons, and maps from the great age of exploration. Don't miss the first sea atlas, the mid-16th century three-masted ship model, or the fine royal sloop—the 'golden coach on water'—last used in 1962 for Queen Juliana's silver wedding anniversary.

The *Amsterdam* The highlight of the museum is moored alongside—the *Amsterdam*, a replica of the 18th-century Dutch East Indiaman that sank off the English coast in 1749 during her maiden voyage. A vivid film *Voyage to the East Indies* is shown, and in summer, actors become bawdy 'sailors', firing cannons, swabbing the decks, loading cargo and enacting burials at sea.

THE BASICS

www.
scheepvaartmuseum.nl

+ J5

✉ Kattenburgerplein 1

☎ 5232222

🕐 Tue–Sun 10–5 (also Mon 10–5, mid-Jun to mid-Sep, and hols). Closed 1 Jan, 30 Apr, 25 Dec. The crew puts on regular re-enactments on board the *Amsterdam* Apr–end Oct, call for details of events and enactments

🍴 Restaurant

🚌 Bus 22, 32, 42, 43

🚤 Museumboat stop 12

♿ Very good

💶 Expensive

❓ Souvenir and book-shop, model-boat kit shop Thu–Sat only, multimedia theatre

Stedelijk Museum CS **TOP 25**

The Stedelijk Museum CS displays modern art while its home (below) is refurbished

THE BASICS

www.stedelijk.nl

🔲 H4

✉ Oosterdokskade 3–5. Note that the museum plans to return to its permanent premises at Paulus Potterstraat 13 by 2008

☎ 5732911

🕐 Daily 10–6

🚉 Centraal Station

🚊 Tram 1, 2, 4, 5, 6, 9, 13, 16, 17, 24, 25

🚤 Museumboat stop 2

♿ Moderate

💷 Expensive

❓ Lectures, films and concerts

HIGHLIGHTS

● *The Parakeet and the Mermaid*, Matisse (1952–53)
● *My Name as Though it were Written on the Surface of the Moon*, Nauman (1986)
● *Sitting Woman with Fish Hat*, Picasso (1942)
● *Beanery*, Kienholz (1965)
● Rietveld furniture collection

One of the world's leading modern art museums. It features Henri Matisse to Kazimir Malevich and Piet Mondrian, and Paul Klee to Vasily Kandinsky and Edward Keinholz.

Controversial The Stedelijk or Municipal Museum, Amsterdam's foremost venue for contemporary art, was founded in 1895. The museum is temporarily housed in the former Post Building, in the old harbour area east of Centraal Station (hence the temporary addition of 'CS' to its name) while its regular home is being refurbished and expanded. Its collection of more than 25,000 paintings, sculptures, drawings, graphics and photographs contains works by some of the great names of modern art (van Gogh, Cézanne, Picasso, Monet, Chagall), but the emphasis is on progressive postwar movements.

House of Museums In 1938 the Stedelijk became Holland's National Museum of Modern Art, but it achieved its worldwide avant-garde reputation in 1945–63, when it was under the dynamic direction of Willem Sandberg. He put much of its existing collection in storage and created a House of Museums in which art, photography, dance, theatre, music and cinema were all represented in innovative shows.

Cutting edge Museum highlights include suprematist paintings by Malevich; works by Mondrian, Gerrit Rietveld and other exponents of the Dutch De Stijl school; and a remarkable collection of almost childlike paintings by the Cobra movement.

More to See

AMSTEL

The river is a busy commercial thoroughfare, with barges carrying goods to and from the port. In town, its bustling banks are lined by houseboats.

🔡 G6 🚊 Tram 3, 6, 7, 9, 10, 14

AMSTELKERK

Squat and wooden, this Calvinist church (1670) was originally meant to be a temporary structure.

🔡 F7 ✉ Amstelveld ⏰ Closed except during 10.30am Sun service 🚊 Tram 4

GROENBURGWAL

This picturesque canal near the Muziektheater was Monet's preferred choice.

🔡 F5 🅜 Nieuwmarkt

HERMITAGE AMSTERDAM

Opened in 2004 in the 17th-century Amstelhof complex as a 'branch' of St. Petersburg's Hermitage Museum. There are changing exhibitions taken from the Russian parent's collection of art, fine art and crafts.

🔡 G6 ✉ Neerlandia Building, Amstelhof, Nieuwe Herengracht 14 ☎ 5308755

⏰ Daily 10–5 🅜 Waterlooplein
🚢 Museumboat stop 3 🚊 Tram 9, 14
♿ Very good 💶 Moderate

HORTUS BOTANICUS

www.hortus-botanicus.nl
With more than 8,000 plant species, Amsterdam's oldest botanical garden (established here in 1682) boasts one of the largest collections in the world. It has spectacular tropical greenhouses, a medicinal herb garden, and an orchid nursery.

🔡 H6 ✉ Plantage Middenlaan 2a
☎ 6259021 ⏰ Feb–end Nov Mon–Fri 9–5, Sat–Sun 10–5; Dec–end Jan closes at 4
🍴 Café 🚊 Tram 6, 9, 14 ♿ Good
💶 Moderate

JODENHOEK

Jewish refugees first came here in the 16th century and settled in the east of the city. Almost the entire district was razed to the ground at the end of World War II, leaving only a few synagogues (▷ 68) and diamond factories as legacy of a once-thriving community.

🔡 G5 🅜 Waterlooplein

THE EAST

★

MORE TO SEE

Boats moored on the Amstel river

Zuiderkerk seen from the picturesque Groenburgwal

MUSEUM VAN LOON

www.museumvanloon.nl

The van Loon family lived in this house during the 19th century holding important positions as city mayors and in the Dutch East India Company. The house and its collection are in fine condition, as is the garden and well worth a visit.

✚ F6 ✉ Keizersgracht 672 ☎ 6245255 🕐 Mar–end May, Jul–end Aug Wed–Mon 11–5; Jun, Oct–end Feb Fri–Mon 11–5 🚊 Tram 16, 24, 25 👋 Inexpensive

MUZIEKTHEATER

www.hetmuziektheather.nl

Amsterdam's theatre for opera and dance is known as the false teeth because of its white marble panelling and redbrick roof. The complex includes the uninspiring buildings of the new town hall (Stadhuis). The design caused great controversy when it was built in 1986, sparking riots during its construction.

✚ G5 ✉ Waterlooplein 22 ☎ 6255455 (recorded informaton in Dutch, hold for operator) 🚇 Waterlooplein 🚊 Tram 9, 14

NATIONAAL VAKBONDSMUSEUM

It is really the building that is of most interest as the museum devoted to trade unionism is perhaps not the most appealing of subjects. The exterior is impressive and its grandiose interior full of designs by leading artists of the day. Sunlight streams through a double roof of yellow and white glass.

✚ H5 ✉ Henri Polaklaan 9 ☎ 6241166 🕐 Tue–Fri 11–5, Sat–Sun 1–5 🚊 Tram 6 nearby on Plantage Parklaan ♿ Good 👋 Inexpensive

NEMO

www.e-nemo.nl

Children will enjoy learning at this impressive hands-on, interactive museum of modern technology. Loads of opportunities to experiment and explore the world of science and computing. The building itself is striking, designed by Italian architect Renzo Piano in 1997. The crowning glory is the roof terrace, lovely to soak up the sun or watch the sunset.

Muziektheater–home to ballet and opera

The copper hull of NEMO

➕ H4 ✉ Oosterdok 2 ☎ 5313233
🕐 Jul–end Aug daily 10–5; Sep–end Jun
Tue–Sun 10–5 (open daily during hols 10–5).
Closed 1 Jan, 30 Apr, 25 Dec 🍴 Café
🚌 Bus 22, 32 ⛴ Museumboot stop 2
♿ Very good 💶 Expensive

PORTUGEES-ISRAËLIETISCHE SYNAGOGE

Holland's finest synagogue, one of the
first of any size in Western Europe. It is
remarkable that this imposing building
escaped destruction in World War II.
➕ G6 ✉ Mr Visserplein 3 ☎ 6245351
🕐 Sun–Fri 10–4 and service on Sat at 9am.
Closed Jewish hols, Sun 10–12
Ⓜ Waterlooplein ⛴ Museumboot stop 3
🚋 Tram 9, 14 💶 Expensive

REGULIERSGRACHT

Seven bridges cross the water here in
quick succession. When on a tour, the
boat will always slow to give you a
view of the identical humped bridges
stretching along the canal. They are
best viewed from the water at night,
with their strings of lights.
➕ F6 🚋 Tram 4, 16, 24, 25

SCHEEPVAARTHUIS

The peculiarly tapered Maritime
House, encrusted with marine decoration, suggests the bow of an ap-
proaching ship. Commissioned by
seven shipping companies in 1912, it
represents one of the most impressive
examples of the architecture of the
Amsterdam School.
➕ G4 ✉ Prins Hendrikkade 108–111
🚌 Bus 22, 42, 43

WATERLOOPLEIN FLEA MARKET

Amsterdam's liveliest market, full of
funky clothes, curiosities and 'antique'
junk.
➕ G5 ✉ Waterlooplein 🕐 Mon–Fri 9–5,
Sat 8.30–5.30 Ⓜ Waterlooplein 🚋 Tram 9

ZUIDERKERK

Holland's first Protestant church
(1614) and indisputably one of the
city's most beautiful. Its designer,
Hendrick de Keyser, lies buried within.
The distinctive tower is 80m (265ft)
high and affords spectacular views.
➕ G5 ✉ Zuiderkerkhof 72 ☎ 5527977
🕐 Call for times Ⓜ Nieuwmarkt

*The unusally shaped
Scheepvaarthuis building*

The soaring spire of Zuiderkerk

Shopping

DE BEESTENWINKEL
A cuddly-toy shop for adults. Ideal for collectors and small gifts.
➕ F5 ✉ Staalstraat 11
☎ 6231805 🚊 Tram 4, 9, 14, 16, 24, 25

CONCERTO
Finest all-round selection of new and used records and CDs to suit all tastes. Good for jazz, classical music and 1950s and '60s hits.
➕ G6 ✉ Utrechtsestraat 52–60 ☎ 6235228
🚊 Tram 4

EDUARD KRAMER
A huge selection of old Dutch tiles, the earliest dating from the 1500s; many rescued from the kitchens of old canal houses. Also ornaments.
➕ E6 ✉ Nieuwe Spiegelstraat 64
☎ 6230832 🚊 Tram 7, 10

GASSAN DIAMONDS
www.gassandiamonds.com
A tour (daily) of the diamond-polishing and cutting workshop leads inevitably to the sales room.
➕ G6 ✉ Wagenstraat 13–17
☎ 6225333 🚉 Waterlooplein
🚊 Tram 4, 9, 14

DE KLOMPENBOER
www.woodenshoefactory.com
Authentic clog factory with the city's largest selection of hand-crafted footwear.
➕ G5 ✉ Sint-Antoniesbreestraat 51
☎ 6230632 🚊 Tram 1, 2, 5, 13, 17

JASKI ART GALLERY
www.jaski.nl
This gallery is in one of the most picturesque streets to browse some of the best galleries and antiques shops in the city. The gallery specializes in painting, sculpture, ceramics and graphic art by the Cobra artists from 1948–1951.
➕ E6 ✉ Nieuwe Spiegelstraat 27–29
☎ 6203939 🚊 Tram 7, 10

Entertainment and Nightlife

BACKDOOR
Leading 'nonhouse' club for R and B, disco, soul, funk and weekly retro theme nights.
➕ G6 ✉ Amstelstraat 32
☎ 6202333 🕐 Thu–Sat 11pm–4am 🚊 Tram 4, 9, 14

CAFÉ HOOGHOUDT
www.hooghoudtamsterdam.nl
This brown bar-cum-proeflokaal is in an old warehouse lined with

traditional stoneware jenever barrels. Tasty Dutch appetizers go with a big selection of liqueurs.
➕ F6 ✉ Reguliersgracht 11
☎ 4204041 🕐 Tue–Sat 4pm–12 🚊 Tram 4, 9, 24, 25

ESCAPE
Amsterdam's largest disco, which can hold 2,000 dancers, has a dazzling light show and superb sound system.

Chemistry on Saturday is the big night it's busy and you must dress smartly.
➕ F6 ✉ Rembrandtplein 11
☎ 6221111 🕐 11pm–4am (Fri–Sat until 5am) 🚊 Tram 4, 9, 14

HOF VAN HOLLAND
Come here for an evening of Dutch folk music and traditional songs.
➕ F6 ✉ Rembrandtplein 5
☎ 6234650 🚊 Tram 4, 9, 14

HOLLAND EXPERIENCE 3-D MOVIE THEATRE
www.holland-exprience.nl
A film tour of Holland's landscape and attractions complete with sights, sounds and smells.
🚇 G5 ✉ Jodenbreestraat 8–10 ☎ 4222233 ⏰ Daily 10–6 🚊 Tram 9, 14
💷 Expensive

JANTJES VERJAARDAG
www.jantjesverjaardag.nl
Cool cocktails and hot dancing—to the latest salsa and *merengue* beats.
🚇 G6 ✉ Amstelstraat 9 ☎ 6251973 ⏰ Fri–Sat 11.30pm–5am, Sun until 4am 🚊 Tram 4, 9, 14

DE KLEINE KOMEDIE
www.dekeinekomedie.nl
The very best cabaret and stand-up comedy, in one of the city's oldest theatres.
🚇 F6 ✉ Amstel 56 ☎ 6240534 🚊 Tram 4, 9, 14

KONINKLIJK THEATER CARRÉ
www.theatercarre.nl
The Royal Theatre hosts long-running international musicals, revues, cabaret, folk dancing and an annual Christmas circus.
🚇 G7 ✉ Amstel 115–25 ☎ 5249452 🚇 Weesperplein

MUZIEKTHEATER
www.hetmuziektheater.nl
An Amsterdam cultural mainstay and home to the Nederlands Opera and the Nationale Ballet since it opened in 1986, The Netherland's largest auditorium, seating 1,689, mounts an international repertoire as well as experimental works from its resident operatic and ballet companies, plus leading international companies. There are guided backstage tours on Wednesday and Saturday at 3pm (▷ 76).
🚇 G6 ✉ Waterlooplein 22 ☎ 6255455 (recorded information in Dutch; hold for operator) 🚇 Waterlooplein

RAIN
www.rain-amsterdam.com
Rain is a great combination of good food, classy cocktails and late-night dancing in chic surroundings. After eating Rain transforms into a nightclub with a blend of global sounds from hip-hop to house.
🚇 F6 ✉ Rembrandtplein 44 ☎ 6267078 ⏰ Sun–Thu 6pm–2am, Fri, Sat 6pm–4am 🚊 Tram 4, 9, 14

ROYAL CAFÉ DE KROON
Affects a cool, hard-edged modernity as if to belie a location on the rambunctious Rembrandtplein. A great enclosed balcony is its saving grace.
🚇 F6 ✉ Rembrandtplein 17 ☎ 6252011 🚊 Tram 4, 9, 14

SCHILLER
An evocative art deco bar enhanced with live piano music. Sophisticated for Rembrandtplein.
🚇 F6 ✉ Rembrandtplein 26 ☎ 6249846 🚊 Tram 4, 9, 14

SINNERS IN HEAVEN
www.sinners.nl
Dress smart for this stylish club, with three floors each with different music. Free before midnight.
🚇 G6 ✉ Wagenstraat 3–7 ☎ 6201375 ⏰ Thu–Sat from 11pm 🚊 Tram 4, 9, 14

TUN FUN
www.tunfun.nl
An indoor playground for children from 1 to 12 years. Slides, ball pools, an inflatable Amsterdam street, trampolines and even a children's disco. Snacks and drinks available. Children must be accompanied by an adult.
🚇 G5 ✉ Mr. Visserplein 7 ☎ 6894300 ⏰ Daily 10–6 🚇 Waterlooplein 🚊 Tram 9, 14

Restaurants

PRICES

Prices are approximate, based on a 3-course meal for one person.

€€€	over €40
€€	€20–€40
€	under €20

CAFÉ DE FLES (€€)

www.defles.nl

Warm cellar full of large wooden tables. A real locals' hangout. The entrance is via Prinsengracht 955.

⊞ F6 ⊠ Vijzelstraat 137, Grachtengordel ☎ 6249644 ⊙ Dinner only ➡ Tram 16, 24, 25

GOLDEN TEMPLE (€)

An imaginative menu of Indian, Mexican and Middle Eastern dishes.

⊞ G7 ⊠ Utrechtsestraat 126, Grachtengordel ☎ 6268560 ⊙ Dinner only ➡ Tram 4

HEMELSE MODDER (€€)

Sophisticated main courses and delicious desserts.

⊞ G4 ⊠ Oude Waal 11, Centrum ☎ 6243203 ⊙ Tue–Sun dinner only 6–10 for last orders ⊛ Nieuwmarkt

INDRAPURA (€€)

www.indrapura.nl

A popular colonial-style restaurant. Tell the waiter how hot and spicy you want your dishes to be. Some of the best *rijsttafel* in town. Special wine list to suit strength of dishes.

⊞ F6 ⊠ Rembrandtplein 40-42, Grachtengordel ☎ 6237329 ⊙ Dinner only ➡ Tram 4, 9, 14

PASTA E BASTA (€€)

www.pastaebasta.nl

Pasta in chic surroundings, which features singing bartenders and waitresses.

⊞ E6 ⊠ Nieuwe Speigelstraat 8, Grachtengordel ☎ 4222222 ⊙ Dinner only ➡ Tram 16, 24, 25

PIET DE LEEUW (€–€€)

Steaks, steaks and yet more steaks are the house specialty at this atmospheric old place, but also some traditional dishes.

⊞ F7 ⊠ Noorderstraat 11, Grachtengordel ☎ 6237181 ⊙ Mon–Fri 12–5, Sat–Sun 5–12 ➡ Tram 16, 24, 25

PINTO (€€)

www.pinto-restaurant.com

This new restaurant is in the Jewish quarter, close to the Joods Historisch

FISH AND VEGETABLES

Although the Dutch eat a lot of meat, Amsterdam with its sea-going associations has a great choice of fish restaurants. Vegetarians, too, have specialty eating places to suit all tastes and budgets, while others, most notably pizzerias and the Asian restaurants around town, offer separate sections in the menus for vegetarian dishes.

Museum, Portuguese synagogue and Waterlooplein. It serves mainly kosher Israeli and French cuisine, plus sandwiches and takeout food. Friendly staff.

⊞ F7 ⊠ Jodenbreestraat 144, Grachtengordel ☎ 6250923 ⊙ Sun–Thu 12–10 ➡ Tram 9. 14

SEA PALACE (€€)

www.seapalace.nl

Advertised as Europe's first floating restaurant, the Sea Palace is modelled on a Chinese pagoda-style palace.

⊞ H4 ⊠ Oosterdokskade 8, Oost & Oosterdok ☎ 6264777 ⊙ Centraal Station

TEMPO DOELOE (€€)

www.tempodoeloerestaurante.nl

One of Amsterdam's best Indonesian restaurants, notable for its western interior, exotic flowers and some of the hottest dishes in town.

⊞ G6 ⊠ Utrechtsestraat 75, Grachtengordel ☎ 6256718 ⊙ Dinner only ➡ Tram 4

LE ZINC... ET LES AUTRES (€€)

Home-style French cuisine in a converted canalside warehouse. Choose from two *prix-fixe* menus, one of which is the chef's surprise, plus a first-class *à la carte* menu.

⊞ F7 ⊠ Prinsengracht 999, Grachtengordel ☎ 6229044 ⊙ Tue–Sat dinner only ➡ Tram 4

A distinct district set apart from the city's historic heart. Not just a bland area of suburbia, but an important cultural area, with museums celebrating Amsterdam's best-known artists close to the main city park.

De Krakeling
Theater

Theater
Bellevue

Leidseplein

De Balie

Holland
Casino

Max Euwe
Centrum

WETERINGSCHANS

Rijksmuseum

**Coster
Diamonds**

**Van Gogh
Museum**

Zuiderbad

**Heineken
Experience**

Concertgebouw

ZUID

NSAUKADE

Marnixstraat

Leidse

Nwe Passeer
brstr

elmersstr

elmersstr

str

kade

Zieseniskade

IJnbaans-

Gracht

IJnbaansgracht

WETERINGSCHANS

H M V
Randwijk-
plantsoen

Den Texstr

N Witsenkade

2e
Weteringdwst

STADHOUDERSKADE

2e J v Campenstr

Quellijn-
straat

Quellijn-
straat

Daniël
Stalpert
straat

Saenredamstr

Gerard
Albert Cuypstraat

Doustraat

F Bol STRAAT

Frans Hals-
straat

Ruysdaelkade

HOBBEMAKADE

Singelgracht

Hobbema-
straat

Museum
straat

Honthorst-
straat

Vossiusstraat

Pieter Corneliszoon Hooftstraat

Jan Luijken straat

P C Hooftstraat

P Potterstraat

Ruysdaelstraat

Teniersstr

Hoochstraat

Ruysdael
straat

V d Veldestr

Vondelstraat

Hobbemastraat

STADHOUDERSKADE

Zandpad

Zandpad

Visscherstr

Spiegelgrachtstr

Concert-
gebouw-
plein

G Metsustr

Moreelse
straat

Maes
straat

J
Vermeer-
plein

Wouwermanstr

A Brouwers
str

Waringen
str

A Pijnakerstr

V
BAERLE
STRAAT

Hondecoeterstr
Maes-
straat

Miens-
straat

R Hart-
plein

C Anthoniszstr

Obrecht-
plein

Bronckhorst-
str

D   E   F

Leidseplein

Amsterdam's liveliest square, Leidseplein, buzzes with life both by day and night

THE BASICS

🔲 E6
✉ Leidseplein
🍴 Restaurants and cafés
🚃 Tram 1, 2, 5, 6, 7, 10, 20
🚢 Museumboat stop 5

HIGHLIGHTS

● American Hotel (1904)
● Stadsschouwburg (1894)
● Street entertainment

This square represents Amsterdam's nightlife at its most vibrant. It is filled with street cafés, ablaze with neon and abuzz with street entertainers.

Party district for centuries During the Middle Ages, farmers on their way to market unloaded their carts here, at the outskirts of the city. At the turn of the 19th century, artists and writers gathered here. In the 1930s Leidseplein was the site of many clashes between political factions, and it became the main site of anti-Nazi rallies during the war. In the 1960s it was the stomping ground of the *Pleiners* (Dutch Mods), and in 1992 it witnessed wild celebrations following local football team Ajax's UEFA Cup victory. Today, despite the constant flow of trams through the square, you are almost sure to find fire-eaters and other street entertainers, both good and bad. By night, dazzling neon lights and crowded café terraces seating more than 1,000 people transform the square into an Amsterdam hot spot, busy until the early hours. Look for two notable buildings, both protected monuments: the distinctive, attractive red-brick Stadsschouwburg (Municipal Theatre (▷ 93), with its wide veranda and little turrets, and the art nouveau Amsterdam-American hotel (▷ 112), with its striking art deco Café Américain (▷ 94).

Winter wonderland Whatever the season, Leidseplein remains one of the city's main meeting places. In winter, when most tourists have departed, it becomes quintessentially Dutch. It is the place to be for New Year's Eve celebrations.

Designed by Petrus Cuypers in 1885, this is the place to view the famous Night Watch

Rijksmuseum

Even in this shruken state, the Rijksmuseum's Masterpieces collection is a glorious evocation of the Dutch Golden Age of the 17th century.

Old Masters Holland's most important museum is operating on a limited basis until 2008, while most of the building is being refurbished. But even when it was fully open, the Rijksmuseum could display only a fraction of its collection. Now it has been reduced to the redesigned Philips Wing, to the rear of the main building. The solution has been to display 400 of the 17th-century Old Masters paintings and other pieces from this period. Pride of place goes to Rembrandt's *The Night Watch* (1642). This vast, dramatic canvas—one of his largest and most famous compositions, portraying an Amsterdam militia company—is a showpiece of 17th-century Dutch art. In other rooms hang more works by Rembrandt and by his pupils. Jan Steen, Johannes Vermeer and Frans Hals also feature prominently. Other treasures include a collection of Delftware and two ingeniously made doll's houses—scaled-down copies of old canal houses, with sumptuous 17th-century period furnishings.

Design masterpiece Although most of the Rijksmuseum building is closed, it's still worthwhile to peruse the architecture, even from a distance. The palatial redbrick building was designed by Petrus Josephus Hubertus Cuypers and opened in 1885. It is mostly in the style known as Dutch neo-Renaissance, but Cuypers slipped in some neo-Gothic touches.

THE BASICS

www.rijksmuseum.nl

⊞ E7

✉ Jan Luijkenstraat 1

☎ 6477000

🕐 Daily 9–6 (Fri until 10pm). Closed 1 Jan

🚊 Tram 2, 5

🚢 Museumboat stop 6

♿ Very good

💶 Expensive

HIGHLIGHTS

● *The Night Watch*, Rembrandt (1642)
● *The Jewish Bride*, Rembrandt (1665)
● *The Milk Maid*, Vermeer (1658)
● *The Love Letter*, Vermeer (1670)
● 17th-century doll houses

Van Gogh Museum

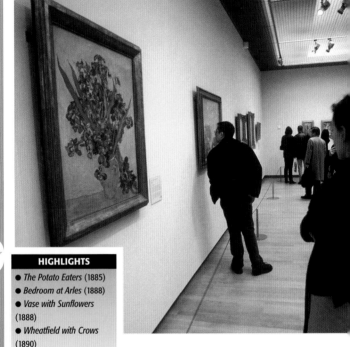

TOP 25

HIGHLIGHTS

● *The Potato Eaters* (1885)
● *Bedroom at Arles* (1888)
● *Vase with Sunflowers* (1888)
● *Wheatfield with Crows* (1890)

TIPS

● Arrive early (9.30am to get in by 10am) or you will find the long lines.
● The best time to visit is Monday morning.

DID YOU KNOW?

● Van Gogh sold only one painting in his lifetime.
● The record price for a van Gogh painting is €37,125 million (1990 *Portrait of Dr. Gachet*).

It is a moving experience to trace Vincent van Gogh's tragic life and extraordinary achievement, through such a varied display of his art, his Japanese prints and his contemporary works.

World's largest van Gogh collection Of his 900 paintings and 1,200 drawings, the van Gogh Museum has 200 and 500 respectively, together with 850 letters, Vincent's fine Japanese prints and works by friends and contemporaries, including Gauguin, Monet, Bernard and Pissarro. Van Gogh's paintings are arranged chronologically, starting with works from 1880 to 1887, a period typified by *The Potato Eaters* (1885).

Artist's palette The broad brush strokes and bold tones that characterize van Gogh's works of

People come from all over to view the most famous pictures by Vincent van Gogh, including the Sunflowers and Irises (left)
The museum houses the largest collection of van Gogh's work anywhere in the world and the building has been specially designed to accommodate his art (right)

1887–90 show the influence of his 1886 move to Paris and the effect of Impressionism, most striking in street and café scenes. Tired of city life, he moved in 1888 to Arles where, intoxicated by the intense sunlight and the brilliant hues of Provence, he painted many of his finest works, including *Harvest at La Crau* and the *Sunflowers* series. After snipping off a bit of his ear and offering it to a local prostitute, van Gogh voluntarily entered an asylum in St.-Rémy, where his art took an expressionistic form. His mental anguish may be seen in the way he painted gnarled trees and menacing skies, as in the desolate *Wheatfield with Crows*. At the age of 37, he shot himself.

Extra space Temporary and special exhibitions are mounted in an ellipse-shape wing by Japanese architect Kisho Kurokawa and opened in 1999.

THE BASICS

www.vangoghmuseum.nl
➕ D7
✉ Paulus Potterstraat 7
☎ 5705200
🕐 Daily 10–6 (Fri until 6pm). Closed 1 Jan
🍴 Self-service restaurant
🚋 Tram 2, 3, 5, 12
🚢 Museumboat stop 6
♿ Excellent
💶 Expensive

Vondelpark

This is a popular place for sunbathers, joggers, Frisbee-throwers and book-worms. Be entertained by street players and acrobats in this welcome splash of green near the heart of the city.

Pleasure gardens With its wide-open spaces, fragrant rose garden, playgrounds, bandstand and cafés, Vondelpark is a popular place of escape from the busy city streets. Amsterdam's largest and oldest municipal park—a 48ha (118-acre) rectangle of former marshland—was first opened in 1865. The designers, J. D. and L. P. Zocher, created an English-style park with lengthy pathways, open lawns, ornamental lakes, meadows and woodland containing 120 varieties of tree. Financed by wealthy local residents, the Nieuwe Park (as it was then called) became the heart of a

The monumental statue of the eponymous Joost van den Vondel takes pride of place in the shady Vondelpark (left)
Only minutes from the hustle and bustle of city life, the Vondelpark provides a haven of green, perfect for relaxation (right)

luxurious new residential district, overlooked by elegant town houses and villas. Two years later, a statue of Holland's best-known playwright, Joost van den Vondel (1587–1679) was erected in the park (▷ 90). It is the only city park in Holland that has been designated a listed monument. There is a small statue dedicated to Kerwin Duinmeyer, a 15-year-old black youth stabbed in 1985. The park is home to the Nederlands Filmmuseum (▷ 93).

Like a summer-long pop festival The heyday of the Vondelpark was in the 1970s, when hippies flocked to Amsterdam, attracted by the city's tolerance for soft drugs. Vondelpark soon became their main gathering place. The bubble burst at the end of the decade and the hippies dispersed. All that now remains are street musicians, flea markets and the occasional ageing hippy.

THE BASICS

✚ B8
✉ Stadhouderskade
🕐 Dawn–dusk
🍴 Café Vertigo (▷ 94), 't Blauwe Theehuis (▷ 92)
🚊 Tram 1, 2, 3, 5, 6, 12, 20
🚤 Museumboat stop 5, 6
♿ Good
❓ Open-air summer festival of theatre and concerts

More to See

CONCERTGEBOUW
www.concertgebouw.nl
The orchestra and main concert hall of this elaborate neoclassical building have been renowned worldwide ever since the inaugural concert in 1888.
➕ D8 ✉ Concertgebouwplein 2–6
☎ 6718345 🕐 Box office daily 10–8.15
🚋 Tram 3, 5, 12, 16, 24

COSTER DIAMONDS
www.costerdiamonds.com
This quality diamond workshop is one of a few in the city to give tours. The diamond business has flourished in Amsterdam since the 16th century. See the diamond cutters at work.
➕ D7 ✉ Paulus Potterstraat 2–8
☎ 3055555 🕐 Daily 9–5 🚋 Tram 2, 5, 20
♿ Few 💷 Free

HEINEKEN EXPERIENCE
www.heinekenexperience.com
An interactive introduction to the world of Heineken beer can be found in the former brewery, an uninspiring building that was producing beer until 1988. You'll see plenty about the process of brewing and old Heineken adverts. Don't miss the stables housing the Shire horses that are still used to pull the drays around Amsterdam. Finally, you'll get your free tasting.
➕ F8 ✉ Stadhouderskade 78
☎ 5239666 🕐 Tue–Sun 10–6; last admissions 5. Closed 1 Jan, 25, 26 Dec 🚋 Tram 4, 6, 7, 10, 16, 24, 25 ♿ Few (call in advance)
💷 Expensive ❓ No under 18

JOOST VAN DEN VONDEL STATUE
Erected in memory of the city's most famous playwright, this elaborate statue presides over the Vondelpark. A contemporary of Rembrandt, Vondel's name was chosen for the park over that of the artist's.
➕ C7 ✉ Vondelpark 🚋 Tram 1, 2, 3, 5, 6, 12, 20 🚤 Museumboat stop 5, 6

DE KRAKELING THEATER
Mime and puppet shows, for under-12s, and over-12s.
➕ D6 ✉ Nieuwe Passeerdersstraat 1
☎ 6245124 🕐 Shows Thu–Sat 8pm, Sun, Wed 2pm 🚋 Tram 7, 10 ♿ Good
💷 Moderate

The neoclassical Concertgebouw

Displays in the Heineken Experience

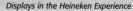

Around the Museums and the Park

This walk enables you to visit some of the most famous museums in the city and also give you the chance to relax in the park.

DISTANCE: 3km (2 miles)   **ALLOW:** 1–2 hours (plus stops)

START

RIJKSMUSEUM
⊞ E7 🚋 Tram 2, 5

END

RIJKSMUSEUM
⊞ E7 🚋 Tram 2, 5

① Start at the park at the back of the Rijksmuseum (▷ 85) by the museum shop. Across the road is Paulus Potterstraat and Coster Diamonds (▷ 90), where you can take a tour.

② Continuing along Potterstraat you will see the cubist Van Gogh Museum (▷ 86–87) on your left. Continue and turn right into Van Baerlestraat.

③ Take the first entrance into the Vondelpark (▷ 88–89), in front of you. Wander through the park and you will see the statue of Joost van Vondel (▷ 90).

④ Make your way back to the original entrance. Continue round the park passing the pavilion that houses the Nederlands Filmmuseum (▷ 93).

⑧ Continue to the junction with Hobbemastraat, where the trams rails cross, and you will find the Rijksmuseum at the end.

⑦ Turn first right onto the main street 1e Constantijn Huygensstraat taking the third left into Pieter Corneliszoon Hoofstraat, one of the most exclusive shopping streets in the city; everything from Gucci to Armani is here.

⑥ This church, reminiscent of Sleeping Beauty's castle was built in 1880. About 100m (100 yards) to the left of the church is the indoor riding school, the Hollandse Manege (▷ 93). Retrace your steps and head down Vondelstarat.

⑤ Leaving the park by the entrance on the right head to the Vondelkerk ahead of you.

Shopping

MEXX
Top designer boutique where you'll find many leading French and Italian labels. The jagged windows of the shop frontage make this the most dramatic in the street.
⊞ D7 ✉ P. C. Hooftstraat 118 ☎ 6750171 ▣ Tram 2, 3, 5, 12

OGER
www.oger.nl
One of the top menswear boutiques and the most conservative choice. Precision made to measure suits can be ordered.
⊞ D7 ✉ P. C. Hooftstraat

MUSEUM SHOPS
Other places to buy art, though not originals, are museum shops that sell high-quality poster reproductions of the famous artworks on their walls, by both Dutch and international artists. Look for the best of these at the Rijksmuseum (a small selection until the whole gallery is reopened in 2008 and at present the shop does get very crowded), Van Gogh Museum, Stedelijk Museum and Museum Het Rembrandthuis.

75–81 ☎ 6768695 ▣ Tram 2, 3, 5, 12

OILILY
Children will likely love the bright and patterned sporty clothes of this Dutch company.
⊞ D7 ✉ P. C. Hooftstraat 131–133 ☎ 6723361 ▣ Tram 2, 3, 5, 12

RETRO
Way-out fashion, including a dazzling array of 1960s and '70s flower-power clothing.
⊞ C6 ✉ Tweede Constantijn Huygensstraat 57 ☎ 6834180 ▣ Tram 1, 3, 6, 12

Entertainment and Nightlife

'T BLAUWE THEE-HUIS
www.blauwetheehuis.nl
This 1930s pagoda-like structure is a popular lunch spot and place to people-watch but it also has a stylish upstairs bar with a DJ starring on Friday evenings in summer.
⊞ B8 ✉ Vondelpark 5 ☎ 6620254 ▣ Tram 1, 3, 12

BOOM CHICAGO
www.boomchicago.nl
Very popular comedy theatre with bar and restaurant. Sketches and improvization, all in English every night, plus late shows in summer.
⊞ E6 ✉ Leidseplein 12

☎ 4230101 ▣ Tram 1, 2, 5, 6, 7, 10

BULLDOG PALACE
www.bulldog.nl
Flagship of the Bulldog chain of bars and smoking coffee shops—brashly decked out in stars and stripes. Downstairs is a 'smoking coffeeshop'.
⊞ E6 ✉ Leidseplein 13–17 ☎ 6271908 ▣ Tram 1, 2, 5, 6, 7, 10

CITY
A multiscreen cinema, just off Leidseplein.
⊞ E6 ✉ Kleine Gartmanplantsoen 15 ☎ 0900 9363 (premium rate) ▣ Tram 1, 2, 5, 6, 7, 10

CONCERTGEBOUW
www.concertebouw.nl
One of the world's finest concert halls, the magnificent neoclassical Concertgebouw has wonderful acoustics, making it special with musicians worldwide. Since its début in 1888, it has come under the baton of Richard Strauss, Mahler, Ravel, Schönberg and Bernard Haitink to name a few. It continues to be one of the most respected ensembles in the world, attracting renowned performers.
⊞ D8 ✉ Concertgebouwplein 2–6 ☎ 6718345 ▣ Tram 3, 5, 12, 16, 24

FISHING

Obtain a permit from the Amsterdam Fishing Federation to fish in the lake in Amsterdamse Bos.
➕ F7 ✉ Nicolaas Witsenstraat 10 ☎ 6264988 🚃 Tram 6, 7, 10

HOLLAND CASINO AMSTERDAM

www.hollandcasino.com
Try all the usual games, plus *Sic Bo* (a Chinese dice game) at this casino, one of Europe's largest. There is a small entrance fee and you must be over 18 and present your passport, but there is no strict dress code.
➕ D6 ✉ Max Euweplein 62 ☎ 5211111 🚃 Tram 1, 2, 5, 6, 7, 10

HOLLANDSCHE MANEGE

Amsterdam's most central riding school, dating from 1882, when the location was positively rural, provides riding in the Amsterdamse Bos.
➕ C7 ✉ Vondelstraat 140 ☎ 6180942 🚃 Tram 1, 6

IN-LINE SKATING

Friday night is skating night, when hundreds turn out for a mass skate from Vondelpark—when the weather is fine enough. Skates can be rented.
➕ B8 ✉ Vondelpark 3 🚃 Tram 1, 3, 12

JOGGING

There are marked trails for joggers through the Vondelpark.

➕ B8 ✉ Vondelpark 3 🚃 Tram 1, 3, 12

NEDERLANDS FILMMUSEUM CINEMATHEEK

www.filmmuseum.nl
On the Vondelpark's northeasrtern corner you will find the imposing pavilion designed by P. J. and W. Hamer in 1881. Movies feature an international agenda and range from silent films to more recent releases. The outdoor veranda is popular in summer for drinks.
➕ C7 ✉ Vondelpark 3 ☎ 5891400 🚃 Tram 1, 3, 12

PARADISO

www.paradiso.com
Amsterdam's best venue for live acts—rock, reggae and pop concerts—in a beautiful old converted church, once the haunt of 1960s hippies.

MELKWEG

Located in a wonderful old dairy building (hence the name Melkweg or 'Milky Way') on a canal just off Leidseplein, this off-beat multimedia entertainment complex opened in the 1960s and remains a shrine to alternative culture. Live bands play in the old warehouse most evenings, and there is also a schedule of unconventional theatre, dance, art and film events. (✉ Lijnbaansgracht 234 ☎ 5318181; www.melkweg.nl).

➕ E7 ✉ Weteringschans 6–8 ☎ 6264521 🚃 Tram 6, 7, 10

REIJNDERS

Brown cafés are typically on tranquil streets; Reijnders is on brash, neon-lighted Leidseplein yet has retained much of its traditional style and look.
➕ E6 ✉ Leidseplein 6 ☎ 6234419 🚃 Tram 1, 2, 5, 6, 7, 10

STADSSCHOUWBURG

www.stadsschouwburg amsterdam.nl
Classical and modern plays form the main repertoire of the stylish, 19th-century Municipal Theatre.
➕ E6 ✉ Leidseplein 26 ☎ 6242311 🚃 Tram 1, 2, 5, 6, 7, 10

SWIMMMING ZUIDERBAD

This historic indoor pool (built 1912) is only a short stroll from the Rijksmuseum and is the perfect place for children to enjoy letting off steam as light relief after all that sightseeing.
➕ E7 ✉ Hobbemastraat 26 ☎ 6781390 🚃 Tram 2, 5

VONDELPARK OPENLUCHTTHEATER

www.openluchttheater.nl
The open-air theatre in the park offers free drama, cabaret, concerts and children's activities from June to August.
➕ B3 ✉ Vondelpark ☎ 4283360 🚃 Tram 1, 2

Restaurants

PRICES

Prices are approximate, based on a 3-course meal for one person.

€€€	over €40
€€	€20–€40
€	under €20

BAGELS & BEANS (€)

Just the place to stop for a break when visiting the Albert Cuypmarkt. Choose from all manner of bagels. Delicious muffins, great coffee and juices. Nice outdoor terrace.

🔒 E8 ⊠ Ferdinand Bolstraat 70, De Pijp ☎ 6721610 ⏰ Mon–Fri 8.30–6, Sat from 9.30, Sun from 10 🚊 Tram 16, 24, 25

BODEGA KEYZER (€€)

An Amsterdam institution, just re-opened after a long period of refurbishment, next door to the Concertgebouw, specializing in fish and Dutch dishes.

🔒 D8 ⊠ Van Baerlestraat 96, Oud Zuid ☎ 6751866 ⏰ Daily 10am–midnight 🚊 Tram 2, 3, 5, 12, 16

CAFÉ AMÉRICAIN (€)

www.amsterdamamericain.com

Artists, writers and bohemians have frequented this grand art deco café, ever since it opened in 1902.

🔒 D6 ⊠ Amsterdam-American Hotel, Leidseplein 26, Grachtengordel ☎ 5563232 ⏰ Daily 7am–1am 🚊 Tram 1, 2, 5, 6, 7, 10

CAFÉ VERTIGO (€€)

Brown café-style surroundings, where menu-dishes occasionally reflect themes in the Film Museum. Lovely terrace.

🔒 B8 ⊠ Vondelpark 3, Oud Zuid ☎ 6123021 ⏰ Mon–Fri 11am–1am, Sat–Sun 10am–1am 🚊 Tram 1, 3, 12

LE GARAGE (€€€)

French regional cuisine at its best at this trendy brasserie in a converted garage near Vondelpark.

🔒 D8 ⊠ Ruysdaelstraat 54–56, Oud Zuid ☎ 6797176 ⏰ Daily lunch, dinner 🚊 Tram 3, 5, 12, 16, 24

DE OESTERBAR (€€)

The seasonal delights of this elegant fish restaurant include herring in May, mussels in June and delicate Zeeland oysters throughout the summer.

A BITE TO 'EET'

Try an *eetcafé* for filling homemade fare—soup, sandwiches and omelets. Remember that kitchens close around 9pm. Browse market stalls for local delicacies. Most bars offer *borrelhapjes* (mouthfuls with a glass)—usually olives, chunks of cheese or *borrelnoten* (nuts with a tasty coating). More substantial *borrelhapjes* are *bitterballen* (bitter balls), fried balls of vegetable paste; and *vlammetjes* (little flames), yummy spicy mini spring rolls.

🔒 E6 ⊠ Leidseplein 10, Grachtengordel ☎ 6232988 ⏰ Daily noon–11 🚊 Tram 1, 2, 5, 6, 7, 10

DE ORIENT (€€)

Dark, opulent restaurant specializing in *rijsttafels*, with more than 20 different sorts, several of them vegetarian, and with 50 years of experience, this is a good introduction to Indonesian tastes.

🔒 D7 ⊠ Van Baerlestraat 21, Oud Zuid ☎ 6734958 ⏰ Dinner only 🚊 Tram 2, 3, 5, 12

SAMA SEBO (€€)

www.samasebo.nl

Rush mats and batik typify this Balinese setting where you can select from the menu to create your own *rijsttafel*.

🔒 D7 ⊠ P. C. Hooftstraat 27, Oud Zuid ☎ 6628146 ⏰ Closed Sun 🚊 Tram 2, 5

SMALL TALK (€€)

Near Museumplein, this *eetcafé* is ideal for snacks between gallery visits.

🔒 D8 ⊠ Van Baerlestraat 52, Oud Zuid ☎ 6714864 ⏰ Mon–Sat 10–9, Sun 10–8 🚊 Tram 2, 3, 5, 12

VAN ALTENA (€)

For the finest Dutch raw herring, other seafood snacks, and even a glass of fine wine, visit this sophisticated stand beside the Rijksmuseum.

🔒 E7 ⊠ Stadhouderskade, at Jan Luijkenstraat, Oud Zuid ☎ 6769139 ⏰ Tue–Sun 11–7 🚊 Tram 6, 7, 10

Just a bus or tram ride will take you into the suburbs with a plethora of windmills, the zoo and more museums. A little farther out it is easy to get to Delft or the Keukenhof Gardens for a pleasant change.

Tropenmuseum

TOP 25

Exhibits from the far flung corners of the earth are on show at the Tropenmusem

THE BASICS

www.kit.nl/tropenmuseum
➕ K7
✉ Linnaeusstraat 2
☎ 5688215; 5688200 recorded info. Children's Museum ☎ 5688233
🕐 Daily 10–5; closed 1 Jan, 30 Apr, 5 May, 25 Dec. Children's Museum Wed afternoons, Sat–Sun and Mon–Fri during school hols
🍴 Ekeko restaurant
🚊 Tram 9, 10, 14, 20
♿ Very good
💶 Expensive
❓ Tropentheater

HIGHLIGHTS

● Bombay slums
● Arabian souk
● Bangladeshi village
● Indonesian farmhouse
● Indonesian gamelan orchestra
● Pacific carved wooden boats
● Papua New Guinean Bisj Poles
● Puppet collection

In the extraordinary Tropical Museum, once a hymn to colonialism, vibrant reconstructions of street scenes with sounds, photographs and slides evoke contemporary life in tropical regions.

Foundations In 1859 Frederik Willem van Eeden, a member of the Dutch Society for the Promotion of Industry, was asked to establish a collection of objects from the Dutch colonies 'for the instruction and amusement of the Dutch people'. The collection started with a simple bow, arrows and quiver from Borneo and a lacquer water scoop from Palembang, then expanded at a staggering rate, as did the number of visitors. In the 1920s, to house the collection, the palatial Colonial Institute was constructed and adorned with stone friezes to reflect Holland's imperial achievements. In the 1970s, the emphasis shifted away from the glories of colonialism towards an explanation of Third World problems. Beside the museum is the Oosterpark, a pleasant green space.

Another world The precious collections are not displayed in glass cases, but instead are set out in lifelike settings, amid evocative sounds, photographs and slide presentations, so that you feel as if you've stepped into other continents. Explore a Bombay slum, feel the fabrics in an Arabian souk, have a rest in a Nigerian bar, contemplate in a Hindu temple or listen to the sounds of Latin America in a café. The Tropentheather, has visiting performers staging non-Western music, theatre and dance in the evenings.

More to See

1100 ROE
This old smock mill, shaped like a peasant's smock, stands 1,100 roes from the city's outer canal. The word *roe* means both the flat part of a sail that had to be set or reefed according to wind strength, and a unit of measurement (about 28cm/1ft) used to calculate the distance from the heart of the city.

✚ Off map at A5 ✉ Herman Bonpad, Sportpark Ookmeer 🚌 Bus 19, 192

1200 ROE
This early 17th-century post mill, with its impressive platform and revolving cap, was built to drain the polders.

✚ Off map at A2 ✉ Haarlemmerweg, near Willem Molengraaffstraat 🚌 Bus 46

ALBERT CUYPMARKT
Amsterdam's biggest, best-known and least expensive general market, named after a Dutch landscape artist, attracts some 20,000 bargain hunters on busy days.

✚ F8 ✉ Albert Cuypstraat 🕐 Mon–Sat 9.30–5 🚊 Tram 16, 24, 25

AMSTELPARK
A formal rose garden and a rhododendron valley are two of the seasonal spectacles at this magnificent park, created in 1972 for an international horticultural exhibition. It also offers pony rides, miniature golf, a children's farm, the Rieker windmill (▷ 101) and other attractions. There is a walk for the blind, and in summer you can tour the park in a miniature train.

✚ Off map at F9 🕐 Dawn–dusk 🍴 Restaurant and café 🚌 Bus 65, 199, 248

AMSTERDAMSE BOS
Amsterdam's largest park was built on the polders outside the city in the 1930s. It is a popular family destination on weekends whatever the season. In winter, there is tobogganing and skating, in summer swimming, sailing and biking. Take a tram ride through the park in antique cars acquired from various European cities.

✚ Off map at A9 ✉ Amstelveen 🕐 24 hours. Visitor centre daily 12–5 🍴 Open-air pancake restaurant and café 🚌 Bus 142, 170, 172 ✋ Free

Sculling down the lake in the Amsterdamse Bos

ARTIS ZOO (NATURA ARTIS MAGISTRA)

www.artis.nl

As well as animals, the complex includes museums, an aquarium and the Planetarium (hourly shows). Ongoing work is continuing to enhance the living conditions of some of the larger animals.

🟦 J6 ✉ Plantage Kerklaan 38–40
☎ 5233400 🕐 Daily 9–5 (6 in summer)
🍴 Restaurant and café 🚋 Tram 6, 9, 14
🚤 Artis Express boat from Centraal Station
♿ Good 💰 Expensive

BEVERWIJKSE BAZAAR

This huge indoor flea market 20km (12.5 miles) northwest of Amsterdam (reputedly Europe's largest) has an Eastern Oriental Market.

🟦 Off map at A1 ✉ Industrieterrein De Pijp, Buitenland 30, Beverwijk 🕐 Sat 8–6, Sun (Eastern Market only) 8–6 🚉 Beverwijk-Oost

DE BLOEM

This old grain mill, built in 1768, re-sembles a giant pepper shaker.

🟦 B2 ✉ Haarlemmerweg, at Nieuwpoortkade 🚌 Bus 18, 46

ENTREPOTDOK

The old warehouses at Entrepotdok have been converted into offices and apartments.

🟦 J5 ✉ Entrepotdok 🚌 Bus 22, 43

DE GOOIER (FUNENMOLEN)

Built on a brick base in 1725, with an octagonal body and a thatched wooden frame, it has been converted into a small brewery and bar.

🟦 K6 ✉ Funenkade 🕐 Wed–Sun 3–8, Fri tour 4pm 🚋 Tram 10; bus 22, 43

KINDERBOERDERIJ DE PIJP

A farm especially for children, south of the city.

🟦 F9 ✉ Lizzy Ansinghstraat 82
☎ 6648303 🕐 Mon–Fri 11–5, Sat–Sun 1–5
🚋 Tram 12, 25 ♿ Few 💰 Free

MOLEN VAN SLOTEN

www.molenvansloten.nl

Tour round this 1847 working mill. Also has a coopery museum.

Line up to see the animals at Artis Zoo

De Gooier windmill

🚩 Off map at A9 ⊠ Akersluis 10 🕐 Daily 10–4 🚻 Good 🚋 Tram 2; bus 145 💷 Moderate

DE PIJP

This lively, multicultural area was once one of Amsterdam's most attractive working-class districts outside the Grachtengordel. The bustling Albert Cuypmarkt takes place daily (▷ 99). Diamond-cutting workshops, too.
🚩 F8 🚋 Tram 16, 20, 24, 25

PLANTAGE

The Plantation became one of Amsterdam's first suburbs in 1848. Before that, this popular and leafy residential area was parkland.
🚩 H5 🚋 Tram 9, 14

DE RIEKER

The finest windmill in Amsterdam was built in 1636 to drain the Rieker polder, and is at the southern tip of the Amstelpark. This was one of Rembrandt's special painting locations. The windmill has been beautifully preserved and is a private home.

🚩 Off map at F9 ⊠ Amsteldijk, near De Borcht 🚋 Bus 248

SARPHATIPARK

A tiny green oasis dedicated to the 19th-century Jewish doctor and city benefactor, Samuel Sarphati.
🚩 F8 🕐 9–dusk 🚋 Tram 3, 25

VERZETSMUSEM (RESISTANCE MUSEUM)

www.verzetsmuseum.org
Rare wartime memorabilia and a fascinating summary of the Dutch resistance during World War II.
🚩 H5 ⊠ Plantage Kerklaan 61a ☎ 6202535 🕐 Tue–Fri 10–5, Sat–Sun 12–5. Closed 1 Jan, 30 Apr, 25 Dec 🚋 Tram 6, 9, 14 🚻 Good 💷 Moderate

WERF 'T KROMHOUT MUSEUM

At one of the city's few remaining working shipyards, this museum documents the development of the Eastern Islands shipbuilding industry.
🚩 J5 ⊠ Hoogte Kadijk 147 ☎ 6276777 🕐 Tue 10–3 🚋 Bus 22, 43 🚻 Few 💷 Inexpensive

★

Smart conversions in the Entrepotdok

Wartime memories in the Verzetsmuseum

Excursions

FARTHER AFIELD

THE BASICS

Distance: 55km (34 miles) southwest
Journey time: 1 hour
🚆 Train from Centraal Station to the Hague then change for Delft
ℹ️ Hippolytusbuurt 4
☎ 015/2154051; 0900 5151555 local; www.delft.nl

DELFT

This charming old town is known the world over for its blue-and-white pottery. In 1652 there were 32 thriving potteries; today there are just three.

William of Orange led his revolt against Spanish rule from the Prinsenhof in Delft. The building now houses the city museum, which includes a collection of rare antique Delftware. Up the stairs you can still see the holes made by the bullets that killed William in 1584. Delft was also the birthplace of the artist Johannes Vermeer (1632–75).

THE BASICS

Distance: 26km (16 miles) southwest
Journey time: 1 hour
🚆 Train from Centraal Station to Leiden then bus direct
✉️ Lisse
☎ 0252/465555

KEUKENHOF GARDENS

These gardens—whose name means 'kitchen gardens'—at the heart of the Bloembollenstreek (bulb-growing region) rank among the most famous in the world.

The showcase site was bought by a consortium of bulb-growers in 1949 who saw the tourist potential. Visit between March and late May, when more than 7 million bulbs are in bloom, laid out in brilliant swathes of red, yellow, pink and blue.

Decorating the Delftware (above). Magnificent blooms at Keukenhof (right)

Shopping

BEETHOVENSTRAAT
www.beethovenstraat
amsterdam.nl
South of the Vondelpark,
this compact street has
some exclusive fashion
shopping and many other
interesting outlets.
➕ D9 ✉ Beethovenstraat
🚋 Tram 5, 24

OTTEN & ZOON
Some Dutch people still
clomp around in wooden
klompen (clogs). This
shop, sells fine wearable
ones as well as souvenirs
to bring home.
➕ F8 ✉ Eerste Van der

Helsstraat 31 ☎ 6629724
🚋 Tram 16, 24, 25

POL'S POTTEN
www.polspotten.nl
A cornucopia of imagina-
tive household fittings,
both house-designed and
imported, ranging from
pottery to furnishings.
➕ M4 ✉ KNSM-laan 39
☎ 493541 🚋 Tram 10, IJtram

SCALE TRAIN HOUSE
Take home a do-it-your-
self windmill or canal
barge kit as a souvenir.
Also model railways.
➕ C5 ✉ Bilderdijkstraat 94

☎ 6122670 🚋 Tram 3, 12,
13, 14

SCHIPHOL PLAZA
The large shopping mall
at the airport has the
longest opening hours in
the city (7am–10pm).
➕ Off map ✉ Schiphol
Airport 🚋 See transport
details ▷ 116

DE WATERWINKEL
www.springwater.nl
A hundred different miner-
al waters to choose from.
➕ E9 ✉ Roelof Hartstraat
10 ☎ 6755932 🚋 Tram 3,
5, 12, 24

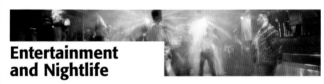

Entertainment and Nightlife

BIMHUIS
www.bimhuis.nl
The place for followers of
avant-garde and experi-
mental jazz, attracting top
international players.
➕ K4 ✉ Muziekgebouw ann
't IJ, Piet Heinkade 3
☎ 7882150 🚋 Tram 16, IJtram

FLEVOPARKBAD
The best outdoor swim-
ming pool in town (mid-
May to late-September).
➕ Off map ✉ Insulindeweg
1002 ☎ 6925030 🚋 Tram 14

GOLFBAAN WATERLAND
www.golfbaanamsterdam.nl
Modern 18-hole golf
course north of the city.

TICKET TIME
From abroad tickets can be
reserved directly through the
Amsterdam Reservations
Centre ☎ 0900 4004040. For
information and tickets, contact the Amsterdam Uit Buro's
Ticketshop (✉ Leidseplein 26
☎ 6211288; www.
amsterdamsuitburo.nl
🕐 Office open daily 10–6,
Thu until 9; phone answered
9–9 daily). Tickets can also be
purchased from the VVV
tourist offices and some
hotels can reserve tickets.
The daily newspapers and
listings magazine *Uitkrant*
have details.

➕ Off map
✉ Buikslotermeerdijk 141
☎ 6361010

ICE SKATING
The canals often freeze in
winter, turning the city
into a big ice rink. Skates
can be bought at most
sports equipment stores.

JAAP EDENBAAN
www.jaapeden.nl
A large outdoor ice rink,
open October to March.
➕ M9 ✉ Radioweg 64
☎ 6949652 🚋 Tram 9

KAMER 401
Relaxed hot-spot in the
Jordaan where you can
have a drink listening to

funky tunes from different DJs. Good place for pre-theatre. Open until late.
🚩 D4 ✉ Marnixstraat 401 ☎ 3204580 🚊 Tram 3, 10

KARTBAAN AMSTERDAM (GO-KARTING)
www.kartbaanamsterdam.nl
Great fun for children large and small.
🚩 Off map ✉ Theemsweg 1, Sloterdijk ☎ 6111642 🚊 Sloterdijk

KORSAKOFF
www.korsakoffamsterdam.nl
Thrash metal and industrial sounds for the chains and piercing crowd—despite which the atmosphere is fun and friendly.
🚩 D5 ✉ Lijnbaansgracht 161 ☎ 6257854 ⏰ Daily from 10pm 🚊 Tram 10, 17

MALOE MELO
www.maloemelo.nl
This smoky yet convivial Jordaan bar, Amsterdam's 'home of the blues', belts out some fine rhythms from some of the best. Occasional jam sessions.
🚩 D5 ✉ Lijnbaansgracht 163 ☎ 4204592 🚊 Tram 3, 10

DE MIRANDABAD
Subtropical swimming pool complex with indoor and outdoor pools, beach, wave machines and a restaurant.
🚩 Off map ✉ De Mirandalaan 9 ☎ 5464444 🚊 Tram 25

MUZIEKGEBOUW AAN 'T IJ
A new star in the city's cultural firmament began to shine early in 2005, with the opening of the Muziekgebouw aan 't IJ. The innovative modern concert hall is an ocean of tinted glass standing on the south shore of the IJ channel, just east of Centraal Station. It is a major international venue for contemporary classical music. There are performances of work by John Cage, Xanakis and other modern music pioneers, and around half the concerts are devoted to modern Dutch compositions. The former Muziekcentrum De IJsbreker experimental music club has moved here, and the Bimhuis jazz club has taken up premises in an annexe.
🚩 K4 ✉ Muziekgebouw aan 't IJ, Piet Heinkade 1 ☎ 7882000 🚊 Tram 26, IJtram

GAY AMSTERDAM
Clubbing is at the heart of Amsterdam's gay scene. The best-known venue is iT, a glitzy disco with throbbing techno. Gay bars and clubs abound in nearby Reguliersdwarsstraat and Halvemaansteeg. To find out exactly what's on and where it's happening, call the Gay and Lesbian Switchboard (☎ 6236565) or read the bilingual (Dutch–English) magazines *Gay News* and *Gay & Night*.

RAI
www.rai.nl
This convention venue sometimes stages classical music and opera.
🚩 Off map ✉ Europaplein 22 ☎ 5491212 🚊 Tram 4

SEASIDE
The seaside is 30 minutes away by train, with miles of clean, sandy beaches. Zandvoort is the closest resort; Bergen aan Zee and Noordwijk are also popular.

SPECTATOR SPORTS
Football (soccer) is Holland's number one spectator sport and the top team is Ajax Amsterdam. Watch them play at their magnificent stadium, the Amsterdam ArenA, (🚩 Off map ✉ Arena Boulevard, Amsterdam Zuidoost ☎ 3111444). Equestrian show-jumping at RAI (🚩 Off map ✉ Europaplein ☎ 5491212) throughout the year, check for details. Jumping Amsterdam is held in April. Look out for a Dutch hybrid of volleyball and netball called *korfball*, and *carambole*—billiards on a table without pockets.

TROPENMUSEUM
Traditional music from developing countries is performed at the museum's Tropentheater (▷ 98).
🚩 K7 ✉ Linnaeusstraat 2 ☎ 5688215 🚊 Tram 6, 9, 10, 14

Restaurants

PRICES

Prices are approximate, based on a 3-course meal for one person.

€€€ over €40
€€ €20–€40
€ under €20

AMSTERDAM (€€)
A beautifully renovated 19th-century water-pumping station is the setting for a cool restaurant, with a menu that's deluge of continental dishes.
✚ D2 ⊠ Watertorenplein 6, Westerpark ☎ 6822666
🚋 Tram 10

LE CIEL BLEU (€€€)
The height of stylish French cuisine on the Okura Hotel's 23rd floor.
✚ F9 ⊠ Ferdinand Bolstraat 333, Nieuw Zuid ☎ 6787450
🕙 Dinner and Sun brunch
🚋 Tram 12, 25

GARE DE L'EST (€€)
In a former station with the policy 'you eat what cook makes'. Mediterranean style. Outdoor terrace.
✚ L5 ⊠ Cruquisusweg 9, Oost ☎ 4630620 🕙 Daily 6–10, Mon–Sat dinner 🚌 Bus 22, 43

DE GOUDEN REAEL (€€€)
French restaurant in a 17th-century dockside building with a romantic waterside terrace. Fine French regional cuisine.
✚ E1 ⊠ Zandhoek 14, Westerdok ☎ 6233883
🚋 Tram 3; bus 35

DE KAS (€€–€€€)
Set in a greenhouse of 1926, this trendy, off-the-beaten-track restaurant serves international dishes with a Mediterranean slant.
✚ K9 ⊠ Kamerlingh Onneslaan 3, Watergraafsmeer ☎ 4624562 🕙 Mon–Fri 12–2, 6.30–10, Sat 6.30–10
🚋 Tram 9

PAKISTAN (€€)
A fine Pakistani restaurant. The menu ranges from traditional, village dishes to highly spiced specialties. It's some way out, southeast of the Vondelpark, but worth it if this is your thing.
✚ Off map ⊠ Scheldestraat 100, Rivierenbuurt
☎ 6753976 🕙 Dinner only
🚋 Tram 12, 25

LA RIVE (€€€)
In Amsterdam's most expensive hotel, chef

SURINAMESE COOKING
Explore the narrow streets of the multiracial district around Albert Cuypstraat, and you will soon realize how easy it is to eat your way around the world in Amsterdam. The many Surinamese restaurants here serve a delicious blend of African, Chinese and Indian cuisine. Specialties include *bojo* (cassava and coconut quiche) and *pitjil* (vegetables with peanut sauce). Check out Marowijne (⊠ Albert Cuypstraat 68–70).

Edwin Kats produces excellent regional French cooking.
✚ G7 ⊠ Amstel Hotel, Prof Tulpplein 1 ☎ 5203264
🕙 Mon–Fri lunch, Mon–Sat dinner 🚋 Tram 6, 7, 10

VIS AAN DE SCHELDE (€€)
www.visaandeschelde.nl
This popular fish restaurant boasts an eclectic menu of fish dishes from around the world. Dine in the art deco interior or out on the patio. Just across the road from the Rai convention venue so you could combine a meal with a visit to the opera or a concert.
✚ Off map ⊠ Scheldeplein 4, Rivierenbuurt ☎ 6751583
🕙 Dinner only 🚋 Tram 4, 12, 24

Delft
SPIJSHUIS DE DIS (€€)
Classy traditional Dutch restaurant where steaks are the specialty.
✚ Off map ⊠ Beestenmarkt 36 ☎ 015/2131782
🕙 Thu–Tue 5–9.50 🚆 Train from Centraal Station to The Hague then change for Delft

STADS PAN-NEKOEKHUYS (€)
You could be spoiled for choice with 90 different types of pancake to choose from here.
✚ Off map ⊠ Oude Delft ☎ 015/2130193 🕙 Apr–Sep daily 11–9 🚆 Train from Centraal Station to the Hague then change for Delft

Amsterdam is probably Europe's most accessible city with plenty of central hotels. It can be hard to find a bargain and checking the Internet and reserving well in advance can be the key.

Where to Stay

Staying in Amsterdam

One of the great attractions of a short break in Amsterdam is that virtually any hotel you consider will be within easy walking distance of all the main attractions. Choosing a hotel on a canal is obviously one of the nicest ideas but you will pay that little bit extra. If you want peace and quiet the Museum District and the area near to the Vondelpark are good options.

Finding a Bargain

Two-fifths of Amsterdam's 30,000 hotel beds are classed as top range properties, making problems for people looking for mid-range and budget accommodation. At peak times, such as during the spring tulip season and summer, empty rooms in lower-cost hotels are about as rare as black tulips. The only answer to this problem is to reserve well ahead. Special offers may be available at other times. Many hotels lower their rates in winter, when the city is quieter than in the mad whirl of summer.

Tips for Staying

Watch out for hidden pitfalls, such as Golden Age canal houses with four floors, steep and narrow stairways and no lift. Most of the canal side hotels are small and only offer bed-and-breakfast. Some low-price options may not offer private bathrooms. Be wary of tranquil-looking mansions with a late-night café's outdoor terrace next door—you may not get a peaceful night.

RESERVATIONS

To be sure to get the rooms you require it is essential to reserve well in advance. Hotels get fully booked months ahead, in particular those with character located along the canals. Low season, November–March, although less popular, still gets booked up as the rates drop by around a quarter. The VVV operates a hotel reservation office Mon–Fri 9–5 ☎ (31) 20 5512512 from outside the Netherlands, ☎ 20 18800 from within. If you do leave it until you arrive the tourist offices make on-the-spot bookings for a small fee.

By the canal or on a street corner, hotels come in all styles and prices in Amsterdam

Budget Hotels

Expect to pay up to €100 for a double room in a budget hotel.

ACACIA

www.hotelacacia.nl
An inexpensive, cheerful, family-run hotel with studio rentals and a pair of houseboats. 14 rooms.
➕ E3 ✉ Lindengracht 251, Jordaan ☎ 6221460
🚋 Tram 3

AGORA

www.hotelagora.nl
Comfortable, 18th-century canal house furnished with antiques and filled with flowers. This hotel couldn't be more central with the Bloemenmarkt close by. 16 rooms.
➕ F6 ✉ Singel 462, Grachtengordel ☎ 6272200
🚋 Tram 4, 9, 14, 16, 24, 25

AMSTEL BOTEL

www.amstelbotel.com
One of Amsterdam's few floating hotels, with magnificent views over the old docks. 175 rooms.
➕ H4 ✉ Oosterdokskade 2–4, Oosterdok ☎ 626424
Ⓜ Centraal Station

ARENA

www.hotelarena.nl
In a handsomely converted 19th-century orphanage, this stylish hotel has a café and restaurant. Dance nights, concerts, exhibitions. 127 rooms.
➕ J7 ✉ 's-Gravesandestraat 51, Oost and Oosterdok
☎ 6947444 🚋 Tram 7, 10

DE FILOSOOF

www.hotelfilosoof.nl
All 25 rooms are named after great philosophers and decorated accordingly. The Vondelpark is close by as are trams to whisk you into the city. Alternatively it is just a 15-minute walk.
➕ C7 ✉ Anna van den Vondelstraat 6, Oud West
☎ 6833013 🚋 Tram 1, 6

NOVA

www.novahotel.nl
A clean, simple, central hotel with friendly young staff in a peaceful location behind the Royal Palace. 61 rooms.
➕ F4 ✉ Nieuwezijds Voorburgwal 276, Centrum
☎ 6230066 🚋 Tram 1, 2, 5

OWL

www.owl-hotel.nl
In a quiet street near Vondelpark, this family-owned hotel has 34 bright rooms and a pretty garden.
➕ D7 ✉ Roemer

There are several campsites in and around Amsterdam. The best-equipped one is a long way out, in the Amsterdamse Bos (✉ Kleine Noorddijk 1, ☎ 6416868). Vliegenbos is just a 10-minute bus ride from the station, close to the IJ waterway (✉ Meeuwenlaan 138, ☎ 6368855; www.vliegenbos.com). Contact the VVV for full details.

Visscherstraat 1, Oud Zuid
☎ 6189484 🚋 Tram 2, 3, 5, 12

PRINSENHOF

www.hotelprinsenhof.com/info
Quaint, comfortable and clean; one of the city's best budget options and on a peaceful canal, too. Quiet area but close to Rembrandtplein with its restaurants, bars and outdoor seating. 11 rooms.
➕ G7 ✉ Prinsengracht 810, Grachtengordel ☎ 6231772
🚋 Tram 4

SINT-NICOLAAS

www.hotelnicolaas.nl
Rambling former factory and comfortable, if sparse, facilities. 24 rooms.
➕ F3 ✉ Spuistraat 1a, Centrum ☎ 6261384
🚋 Tram 1, 2, 5, 6, 13, 17

STAYOKAY AMSTERDAM VONDELPARK

www.stayokay.nl
A wide range of modern options, from dormitories to family rooms. 536 beds.
➕ D7 ✉ Zandpad 5, Vondelpark, Oud Zuid
☎ 5898996 🚋 Tram 1, 2, 5, 6, 7, 10

VAN OSTADE BICYCLE HOTEL

www.bicyclehotel.com
Small hotel that rents bikes to discover hidden Amsterdam. Maps are on offer as well as alternative routes to explore the city on two wheels. 16 rooms.
➕ F9 ✉ Van Ostadestraat 123, De Pijp ☎ 6793452
🚋 Tram 3, 12, 25

Mid-Range Hotels

PRICES

Expect to pay between €100 and €200 for a double room in a mid-range hotel.

AMBASSADE

www.ambassde-hotel.com
Amsterdam's smartest B&B, in ten 17th-century gabled canal houses. Louis XIV-style furniture adds elegance to the 59 bedrooms.
➕ E5 ✉ Herengracht 341, Grachtengordel ☎ 5550222
🚊 Tram 1, 2, 5

AMSTERDAM

www.hotelamsterdam.nl
Fully modernized behind its 18th-century façade, on one of the city's busiest tourist streets. 80 rooms.
➕ F4 ✉ Damrak 93–94, Centrum ☎ 5550666
🚊 Tram 4, 9, 14, 16, 24, 25

AMSTERDAM HOUSE

www.amsterdamhouse.com
Quietly situated small hotel beside the Amstel. Most rooms have a view of the river. 16 rooms. Apartments and houseboat rentals available.
➕ F5 ✉ 's-Gravelandseveer 7, Centrum ☎ 6246607
🚊 Tram 4, 9, 14, 16, 24, 25

ATLAS

www.hotelatlas.nl
Nicely situated on the edge of the Vondelpark, this attractive art nouveuau hotel provides a relaxing stay away from the bustle of the city.

However, the popular and lively Leidseplein is only a short walk away. The top-class museums are also nearby, as is the chic designer shopping street P. C. Hooftstraat. 23 rooms.
➕ C8 ✉ Van Eeghenstraat 64, Oud West ☎ 6766336
🚊 Tram 2, 3, 12

BILDERBERG GARDEN

www.gardenhotel.nl
In a pleasant leafy sub-urb, a short tram ride from the heart of the city. 98 rooms. It's top of the range but check it out for special deals off-season.
➕ C9 ✉ Dijsselhofplantsoen 7, Oud Zuid ☎ 5705600
🚊 Tram 16

BILDERBERG JAN LUYKEN

www.janluyken.nl
A well-run, elegant town-house in a quiet back

ONLINE

One of the best ways to check into Amsterdam is via the Internet and there are some good websites to point you in the right direction. The official sites of the Amsterdam Tourist Board is a good place to start: www.visitamsterdam.nl and www.holland.com (▷ 115). Other specific hotel sites are www.amsterdam-hotels.org (▷ 115) and www.amster-dam.info/hotels. You will also find information if you want to take a trip outside the city.

street near Vondelpark and Museumplein not far from the Van Gogh Museum. 65 rooms.
➕ D7 ✉ Jan Luijkenstraat 58, Oud Zuid ☎ 5730730
🚊 Tram 2, 3, 5, 12

CANAL HOUSE

www.canalhousehotel.com
Antique furnishings and a pretty garden make this small, family-run hotel a gem. The 26 rooms are all maintained in a classic 17th-century style.
➕ E4 ✉ Keizersgracht 148, Grachtengordel ☎ 6225182
🚊 Tram 6, 13, 14, 17

CROWNE PLAZA AMSTERDAM CITY CENTRE

www.amsterdam-citycentre.crowneplaza.com
Centrally located, well-fur-nished hotel with a good range of facilities. At the top end of the mid-price range, with a roof-top terrace, swimming pool and gym. Boasts a good restaurant with Dutch cuisine, De Roode Leeuw (▷ 63). 270 rooms.
➕ F4 ✉ Nieuwezijds Voorburgwal 5, Centrum ☎ 6200500 🚊 Tram 4, 9, 14, 16, 24, 25

ESTHERÉA

www.estherea.nl
A well-considered blend of wood-panelled canal-side character with effi-cient service and modern facilities. It has been in the same family for three generations. Warm and inviting and nice views of the canal. 71 rooms.

E5 ✉ Singel 303–309, Grachtengordel ☎ 6245146 🚊 Tram 1, 2, 5

ITC
www.itc-hotel.com
A quiet gay-orientated, hotel, with a garden, on one of the city's most beautiful canals. 20 rooms.
G7 ✉ Prinsengracht 1051, Grachtengordel ☎ 6230230 🚊 Tram 4

LLOYD HOTEL
www.lloydhotel.com
In a refurbished monument of Amsterdam School architecture from 1921, this innovative hotel opened in 2004 in the harbour redevelopment zone. 116 rooms.
L4 ✉ Oostelijke Handdelskade 34, Oostelijke Eilanden ☎ 5613636 🚊 Tram IJtram

MAAS
www.hotelmaas.nl
A charming, family-run, waterfront hotel near museums, shops and nightlife. 28 rooms.
D6 ✉ Leidsekade 91, Grachtengordel ☎ 6233868 🚊 Tram 1, 2, 5, 6, 7, 10

NH CITY CENTRE
www.nh-hotels.com
This hotel with its striking Amsterdam School-style architecture has particularly good facilities for visitors with disabilities. At the top end of the mid-range hotels, check it out for some excellent out-of-season deals. 209 rooms.
E5 ✉ Spuistraat 288–292,

Centrum ☎ 4204545 🚊 Tram 1, 2, 5

NH DOELEN
www.nh-hotels.com
Amsterdam's oldest hotel, where Rembrandt painted the *Night Watch*; 85 small well-equipped rooms.
F5 ✉ Nieuwe Doelenstraat 24, Centrum ☎ 5540600 🚊 Tram 4, 9, 14, 16, 24, 25

NH SCHILLER
www.nh-hotels.com
Built in 1912, this hotel situated in the popular Rembrandtplein with its bars, restaurants and outdoor café terraces, opitimizes the art deco period. The renovation of the rooms is sympathetic, retaining many of the original elements. The Brasserie Schiller offers both traditional and contemporary cuisine and its art deco interior makes it

---
ALTERNATIVES

If you want to rent an apartment in Amsterdam, contact Amsterdam House (☎ 6262577; www.amsterdamhouse.com); you can take your pick of luxury apartments in converted canal houses, or even a houseboat. Bed and Breakfast Holland (✉ Theophile de Bockstraat 3 ☎ 6157527; www.bedandbreakfast.nl) will set you up with a room in a private house.

the perfect place for afternoon tea or pre-dinner drink. The art collection of Mr Frits Schiller is particularly fine. 92 rooms.
F6 ✉ Rembrandtplein, Grachtengordel 26–36 ☎ 5540700 🚊 Tram 4, 9, 14

PRINS HENDRIK
www.hotel-prinshendrik.nl
Opposite Centraal Station, the Prins Hendrik offers a warm welcome and newly renovated rooms all with bathrooms. Some rooms have great views of the Amsterdam skyline. Cosy bar and restaurant. 39 rooms.
G4 ✉ Prins Hendrikkade 52–58, Centrum ☎ 6237969 🚇 Nieuwmarkt 🚊 All trams to Centraal Station

SEVEN BRIDGES
Small and exquisite; the owners treat their guests like friends. With its position on the city's prettiest canal, this is everyone's special bed-and-breakfast with many guests returning. 11 rooms.
F7 ✉ Reguliersgracht 31, Grachtengordel ☎ 6231329 🚊 Tram 4

VONDEL
www.hotelvondel.com
A boutique hotel dating from 1903 inside five houses in a quiet street near the Vondelpark. Very convenient for Leidseplein and the museums. The 67 rooms are stylish.
D7 ✉ Vondelstraat 28–30, Oud West ☎ 6120120; fax 685 4321 🚊 Tram 1, 6

Planning Ahead

When to Go

Most tourists visit Amsterdam between April and September; late March to late May is the time to see tulips in bloom. June brings the Holland Festival of art, dance, opera and theatre. Although winter can be cold and damp, December is crowded with Christmas shoppers and those staying for the festive season.

TIME

Amsterdam is one hour ahead of London, six hours ahead of New York and nine hours ahead of Los Angeles.

AVERAGE DAILY MAXIMUM TEMPERATURES

JAN	FEB	MAR	APR	MAY	JUN	JUL	AUG	SEP	OCT	NOV	DEC
41°F	43°F	48°F	55°F	63°F	68°F	72°F	72°F	68°F	57°F	46°F	41°F
5°C	6°C	9°C	13°C	17°C	20°C	22°C	22°C	20°C	14°C	8°C	5°C

Spring (March to May) is at its most delightful in May—with the least rainfall and the crowds not so intense as the summer months.

Summer (June to August) is the sunniest of the year but good weather is never guaranteed.

Autumn (September to November) gets wetter, although September is a popular time to visit. The weather is often chilly and drizzly as winter approaches.

Winter (December to February) can be cold, and temperatures can drop so low that the canals freeze. Strong winds can increase the chill factor, and fog can blot out the sunlight for days.

WHAT'S ON

February *Chinese New Year*: In Chinatown (around Zeedijk).
Carnival: Celebrated as a preamble to Lent.

March *Stille Omgang* (2ndSun): Silent procession.

April *National Museum Weekend* (2nd week): Museums lower entrance fees.
Koninginnedag (30 Apr): The official Queens' birthday and day of celebrations.

May *Remembrance Day* (4 May): Pays tribute to World War II victims.

Liberation Day (5 May): Marking the end of the German Occupation in 1945.
National Windmill Day (2nd Sat).
National Cycling Day (2nd Sun).

May/June *Grachetenloop canal race* (last Sun in May or first Sun in June)

June *Holland Festival*: International arts festival.

August *Amsterdam Pride* (early Aug): one of Europe's biggest gay festivals with the spectacular Canal Parade.
Grachtenfestival (mid-Aug):

this annual canal festival culminates with the *Prinsengracht-concert*, classical music recitals on barges outside the Hotel Pulitzer.

September *Bloemencorso* (first Sat): Flower-laden floats from Aalsmeer to Amsterdam.
National Monument Day (2nd Sat): Buildings open.
Jordaan Folk Festival (2nd week): Music, street parties.

November *Sinterklaas* (Santa Claus) Parade (mid-Nov).

December *Oudejaarsavond* (31 Dec): Street parties, fireworks.

Useful Websites

www.channels.nl

Use this website to take a virtual walk around the city. Pick any street and the site will display photographs and links to hotels, museums, shops or restaurants on that street. The forum is full of useful hotel and restaurant reviews written by visitors to Amsterdam.

www.amsterdam-hotels.org
www.holland-hotels.com

Accommodation: The first site represents a cross-section of hotels in the city, from budget to deluxe, including apartments and houseboats. The second covers the whole of the Netherlands, and is useful if you want to travel farther afield or find hotels in nearby towns when all the hotels in Amsterdam are full. Both sites have up-to-date details of tariffs, special offers and room availability, with pictures of typical rooms on offer and maps showing the precise location.

www.visitamsterdam.nl; www.amsterdam.info; www.holland.com

Official tourist board sites: The first two cover Amsterdam and the third the whole of the Netherlands. They are good for information about exhibitions, events and festivals. Both have online hotel booking.

www.dinnersite.nl

Say what kind of food you like and you'll get a comprehensive list of Amsterdam restaurants to suit. More than 9,000 restaurants are featured on this site, covering all the Netherlands, and you can specify criteria such as 'child friendly', 'smoke free', or 'wheelchair accessible'. You can also use the site to make reservations online.

www.bmz.amsterdam.nl

For everything you could ever want to know about the architecture in Amsterdam, visit this excellent and informative site belonging to Amsterdam Heritage.

PRIME TRAVEL SITES

www.eurostar.com
For details of international rail services.

www.ns.nl
Journey planner for getting around Holland by train.

www.hollandsepot.dordt.nl
Fascinating information (mostly in Dutch) on traditional Dutch food, with recipes.

www.fodors.com
A complete travel-planning site. You can research prices and weather; book air tickets, cars and rooms; pose questions (and get answers) to fellow travellers; and find links to other sites.

INTERNET CAFÉS

EasyInternetcafé
www.easyeverything.com
✉ Reguliersbreestraat 22 and at Damrak 33 🕐 Daily 9am–10pm

Freeworld Internet Café
www.freeworld-internet-cafe.nl
✉ Kort Nieuwendijk 30
🕐 Daily 10am–midnight

The Mad Processor
www.madprocessor.nl
✉ Kinkerstraat 11–13
🕐 Tue–Sun 2pm–midnight

Getting There

VISAS AND TRAVEL INSURANCE

For the latest passport and visa information, look up the British embassy website at www.britishembassy. gov.uk or the United States embassy at www.american embassy. com/europe. EU citizens can obtain health care with the production of the EHIC card. However, insurance to cover illness and theft is strongly advised.

DRIVING

If you do bring a car you can follow the excellent electronic signage for parking as you come into the city but be prepared there is often a shortage. Driving is not an ideal way of getting about the city because of the scarcity and high cost of public parking, the one-way narrow and congested streets and the large number of cyclists. Cars are generally discouraged and any penalities incurred will be high. During the annual Queen's Day celebrations around 30 April, many city roads are closed to traffic. Never drive under the influence of alcohol.

AIRPORTS

There are direct international flights into Schiphol Airport from around the world, as well as good rail connections with most European cities and regular sailings from the UK to major ferry ports, all of which have good rail connections to Amsterdam.

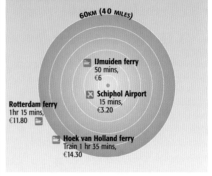

60KM (40 MILES)

IJmuiden ferry
50 mins,
€6

Schiphol Airport
15 mins,
€3.20

Rotterdam ferry
1hr 15 mins,
€11.80

Hoek van Holland ferry
Train 1 hr 35 mins,
€14.30

FROM SCHIPHOL

Schiphol (☎ 0900/0141; www.schiphol), Amsterdam's only international airport, is 13km (8 miles) southwest of the heart of the city. Many international airlines operate scheduled and charter flights here. Trains leave the airport for Amsterdam Centraal Station every 10 minutes from 6am until midnight, then hourly through the night. The ride takes 20 minutes and costs €3.40. Connexxion buses run from the airport to more than 100 hotels and you can request a hotel if it is not on the list. The cost is €12 one way, €19 return; 6am–9pm (☎ 038 3394741). You should never have to wait more than 30 minutes for a bus and they can be every 10 minutes. It leaves outside Arrivals 2. Taxis are available but fares run as high as €50. It is usually faster to go by train to Centraal Station and take a taxi from there.

ARRIVING BY RAIL

Centraal Station has direct connections from major cities in western Europe, including high-speed links from Paris, Brussels and Cologne. From Britain, there are connections at Brussels

with trains operated by Eurostar, with bargain through fares to Amsterdam. Train information: (☎ 0900/9296; www.ns.nl).

CENTRAAL STATION

Wherever you come from be it the airport or the sea-rail connection from Harwich via Hook of Holland you will end up at this station, quite a monument in itself (▷ 51). A few tips can help you avoid problems on arrival:

● Once off the platforms you will find the main concourse is crowded with travellers and loiterers.

● The station is vunerable to pickpockets and hustlers who target tourists.

● Don't be tempted to buy tickets if approached, on the pretext the tickets will be cheaper, they won't be—stick to the automatic ticket machines.

● Tourist information can be found down the stairs on Platform 2A.

● Heading out of the main entrance you will be confronted with a confusion of taxis, trams and scores of bicycles.

● The main taxi rank is to the right of the main entrance as are tram stands 1, 2, 5, 13 and 17.

● To the left are tram stands 4, 9, 16, 24 and 25 and the entrance to the Metro.

● Just beyond is the city's main tourist office in a white-painted wooden building.

● To the left is the GVB, public transport office, where you buy any number of travel passes and reserve tickets for canal cruises (🕒 Mon–Fri 7am–9pm, Sat, Sun 8am–9pm).

ARRIVING BY SEA

The major ferry ports—IJmuiden (23km/14 miles), Rotterdam Europoort (70km/43 miles) and Hoek van Holland (Hook of Holland, 68km/42 miles)—have good rail connections with Amsterdam. Regular sailings from the UK are offered by Stena Line (☎ 08705 707070; www.stenaline.co.uk), DFDS Seaways (☎ 08708 520524; www.dfds.co.uk) and P&O Ferries (☎ 08705 980545; www.poferries.com).

CUSTOMS

Allowances (17 years up) Goods Bought Outside the EU (Duty-Free Limits):
Alcohol: 1 litre of spirits over 22% volume, OR 2 litres of fortified wine, sparkling wine or other liqueurs, PLUS 2 litres of still table wine
Tobacco: 200 cigarettes, OR 100 cigarillos, OR 50 cigars, OR 250g of tobacco
Perfume: 50ml
Toilet water: 250ml

Goods Bought Inside the EU for Your Own Use (Guidance Levels):
Alcohol: 10 litres of spirits AND 20 litres of fortified wine, sparkling wine or other liqueurs, AND 90 litres of wine, AND 110 litres of beer
Tobacco: 800 cigarettes, AND 400 cigarillos, AND 200 cigars, AND 1kg of tobacco

Not allowed:
Drugs, firearms, ammunition, offensive weapons, obscene material, unlicensed animals including birds and insects

---

CAR RENTAL

You will find the usual leading international rental companies both at Schiphol Airport and in the city.

Getting Around

VISITORS WITH DISABILITIES

The Netherlands is one of the most progressive countries in the world when it comes to providing access and information. Hotels, museums and buildings that meet minimum standards display the International Accessibility Symbol. Tourist Information Offices have full information on hotels, restaurants, museums, tourist attractions and boat and bus excursions with facilities for people with disabilities. A special taxi service is available daily 24 hours for people with disabilities (☎ 6333943); reserve at least two days ahead. For further information contact the Federatie Nederlandse Gehandicaptenraad, Postbus 169, 3500 AD, Utrecht (☎ 030 2916600; www.cg-raad.nl).

CANAL TRAVEL

You can buy an all-day ticket for the Canal Bus although the route and schedules are not too easy to follow. The Museumboot operates from Centraal Station and stops at seven tourist points around the city. Water taxis have to be reserved in advance and are expensive. See panel opposite for more details.

Amsterdam has excellent public transportation. Distances are short so you can walk or bicycle to most places. But on a cold, wet day you may be grateful to ride, and a tram trip is an attraction in its own right.

TRAMS AND BUSES

Seventeen different tram lines have frequent services from 6am on weekdays (slightly later on weekends) until 12.30am, when night buses take over, running hourly until 7.30am. Day tickets are valid during the night following the day on which they were issued. It is best to buy your ticket in advance but for a single journey you can pay the conductor. Take care when getting off; many stops are in the middle of the road. There are more than 30 bus routes.

METRO

There are four Metro lines, three terminating at Centraal Station, used mainly by commuters from the suburbs. The most useful city stations are Nieuwmarkt and Waterlooplein.

TAXIS

It is difficult to hail a taxi in the street. Go to a taxi stand at major squares, and outside major hotels, tourist attractions and Centraal Station. Taxis are free to charge what they like, so it is essential to ask the driver for an estimate for the journey before you start. Fares are high. Most passengers round up fares, but it is not customary to give a large tip.

TICKETS

● The same ticket is valid for tram, bus and Metro. If you intend to use public transport frequently, buy a strip ticket (*strippenkaart*) at Amsterdam's municipal transport authority, GVB and Dutch Railways desks at most stations, and also at the Vereniging voor Vreem-delingenverkeer (VVV) tourist offices (▷ 122).

● Having bought your strip of tickets be aware that for each ride, a strip must be used for

each zone you want to pass through, plus one for the ride: For example, from Centraal Station to Leidseplein is one zone, so you need to count down two strips of your *strippenkaart*, and stamp the second one. Zones are shown on maps at tram, bus and Metro stops.

● On buses: Tell the driver the number of zones you want and your ticket will be stamped.

● On the Metro: Before boarding, fold back the appropriate number of strips and punch your ticket in the yellow ticket machines before entering the platform.

● On trams: Either ask the driver to stamp your ticket or do it yourself in a yellow punch-machine.

● For a single trip, purchase a single (1- or 2-zones) ticket, from the driver or conductor of the bus or tram, or from a machine at the Metro entrance. Buy day and other tickets, 2-, 3-, 8-, 15- and 45-strip cards from Metro, and train station ticket counters, VVV offices and newsagents (not all kinds of tickets are available from each of these sources).

● All city-zones single tickets and strips are valid for one hour after the time stamped on them, and include transfers.

● Don't travel without a valid ticket: You could be fined €30 on the spot.

● For further information and maps, contact GVB Tickets & Info ✉ Stationsplein ☎ 0900/9292; www.gvb.nl

GETTING AROUND BY BICYCLE

● The best way to see Amsterdam is by bicycle and the city is geared up to riders on two wheels. There are penty of cycle lanes, distances are short and there are no hills. If you are not used to riding in a city, start on a quiet Sunday to gain confidence.

● To rent a bike costs from €7 a day, €30 a week. Damstraat Rent-a-Bike ✉ Damstraat 20–22 ☎ 6255029; www.bikes.nl ⏰ Daily 9–8. Bike City ✉ Bloemgracht 68–70 ☎ 6263721; www.bikecity.nl ⏰ Daily 9–6.

ORGANIZED SIGHTSEEING

Canal boats are not a part of the public transporation system and although quite expensive are a wonderful way to see the city.

Holland International
✉ Prins Hendrikkade 33a
☎ 6253035. Cruises every 20 minutes in summer; every 30 minutes in winter.

Canal Bus
✉ Weteringschans 24
☎ 6239886; www.canal.nl
Water-bus service around the city. Hop on-and-off day pass is a good option.

Lovers
✉ Prins Hendrikkade opposite 25, near Centraal Station
☎ 5301090; www.lovers.nl
Tours daily 10–5, every 30 minutes.

Museumboot
✉ Stationsplein 8
☎ 5301090; www.lovers.nl
7 stops linking the major museums. Service every 30–45 minutes.

OTHER OPTIONS
Bicycle Tours
Yellow Bike Tours
✉ Nieuwezijds Kolk 29
☎ 6206940; www.yellow-bike.nl

Walking tours
Mee in Mokum
✉ Keizersgracht 346
☎ 6251390. Tours Mon–Fri 1–4.

Essential Facts

MONEY

The euro is the official currency of the Netherlands. Bank notes in denominations of 5, 10, 20, 50, 100, 200 and 500 euros and coins in denominations of 1, 2, 5, 10, 20 and 50 cents and 1 and 2 euros were introduced on 1 January 2002.

10 euros

50 euros

200 euros

500 euros

MONEY MATTERS

Banks may offer a better exchange rate than hotels or independent bureaux de change. GWK (Grenswisselkantoor) offer 24-hour money-changing services at Schiphol Airport and extended hours at Centraal Station.

ELECTRICITY

● 220 volts; round two-pin sockets.

MEDICINES

● For nonprescription drugs, and so on, go to a *drogist*. For prescription medicines, go to an *apotheek*, most open Mon–Fri 8.30–5.30.
● Details of pharmacies open outside normal hours are in the daily newspaper *Het Parool* and all pharmacy windows.
● The Central Medical Service (☎ 5923434) can refer you to a duty GP or dentist.
● Hospital outpatient clinics are open 24 hours a day. The most central is Onze-Lieve-Vrouwe Gasthuis ✚ J7 ✉ 's Gravesandeplein 16 ☎ 5999111 🚊 Trams 3, 10, 17.

NATIONAL HOLIDAYS

● 1 January; Good Friday, Easter Sunday and Monday; 30 April; Ascension Day; Pentecost and Pentecost Monday; 25 and 26 December.
● 4 and 5 May—Remembrance Day (*Herdenkingsdag*) and Liberation Day (*Bevrijdingsdag*)—are World War II Commemoration Days but not public holidays.

NEWSPAPERS AND MAGAZINES

● The main Dutch newspapers are *De Telegraaf* (right wing), *De Volkskrant* (left wing) and *NRC Handelsblad*.
● The main Amsterdam newspapers are *Het Parool* and *Nieuws van de Dag*.
● Listings magazines: *Amsterdam Day by Day* and *Uitkrant*.
● Foreign newspapers are widely available.

OPENING HOURS

● Banks: Mon–Fri 9 until 4 or 5. Some stay open Thu until 7.
● Shops: Tue–Sat 9 or 10 until 6, Mon 1 to 6. Some open Thu until 9 and Sun noon until 5. Some close early Sat, at 4 or 5.
● State-run museums and galleries: most open Tue–Sat 10 to 5, Sun and national holidays 1 to 5. Many close on Mon.

PLACES OF WORSHIP

● Roman Catholic: Parish of the Blessed Trinity, Heilige Familie-kerk: ✉ Zouiersweg 180 ☎ 4652711
● English Reformed Church: ✉ Begijnhof 48 ☎ 6249665
● Jewish: Jewish and Liberal Community Amsterdam: ✉ Jacob Soetendorpstraat 8 ☎ 6423562
● Muslim: Moskee Djame Masdjied Taibah: ✉ Kraaiennest 125 ☎ 6982526; www.taibah.nl

POST OFFICES

● Most post offices open weekdays 8.30 or 9 until 5.
● Main Post Office: ➕ E4 ✉ Hoofdpostkantoor TPG, Singel 250–256 ☎ 5563311 ◉ Mon–Fri 9–6 (Thu 9–8), Sat 10–1.30.
● Postal Information: ☎ 0800/0417
● Purchase stamps (postzegels) at post offices, tobacconists and souvenir shops.
● Post boxes are bright red and clearly marked 'TPG POST'.

TELEPHONES

● Most public telephones take phonecards available from telephone hubs, post offices, rail stations and newsagents.
● Phone calls within Europe cost about €0.35 per minute.
● National directory enquiries: ☎ 0900/8008
● International directory enquiries: ☎ 0900/8418
● Numbers starting 0900 are premium rate calls; 0800 are free; 0600 are mobile phone numbers.
● Local/international operator: ☎ 0800/0410
● To phone abroad, dial 00 then the country code (UK 44, US and Canada 1, Australia 61, New Zealand 64, Ireland 353, South Africa 27), then the number.
● Most hotels have International Direct Dialling, but it is expensive.
● The code for Amsterdam is 020. To phone from outside Holland drop the first 0.

STUDENTS

For discounts at some museums, galleries, theatres, restaurants and hotels, students under 26 can obtain an International Young Person's Pass (CJP–Cultureel Jongeren Pass), cost €12.50 from: AUB ✉ Leidseplein 26 ☎ 0900/0191

LOST PROPERTY

● For insurance purposes, report lost or stolen property to the police as soon as possible.
● Main lost property offices: Centraal Station ➕ G3 ✉ Stationsplein 15 ☎ 5578544 ◉ Daily 7am–11pm
● Police Lost Property ➕ J9 ✉ Stephensonstraat 18 ☎ 5593005 ◉ Mon–Fri 12–3.30
● For property lost on public transport, GVB ➕ G4 ✉ Prins Hendrikkade 108–14 ☎ 0900 8011 ◉ Mon–Fri 9–4

SENSIBLE PRECAUTIONS

● Pickpockets are common in busy shopping streets and markets, and in the Red Light District. Take sensible precautions and remain on your guard at all times.

● At night, avoid poorly lighted areas and keep to busy streets. Amsterdam is not dangerous, but muggings do occur.

● There are no particular risks to women travelling alone. Wearing a wedding ring can help deter unwanted attention.

TOILETS

● There are few public toilets. You're best bet is to use the facilities in museums and department stores. There is often a small charge (€0.30–€0.50).

TOURIST OFFICES (VVV)

● The three Vereniging voor Vreemdelingenverkeer (VVV) offices and the Holland Tourism International desk at Schiphol Airport all have multilingual staff (all offices ☎ 2018800; www.visitamsterdam.nl). They will also make hotel, excursion, concert and theatre reservations for a small fee.
They are:
Centraal Station VVV ✚ G3 ☒ Centraal Station, Platform 2
Stationsplein VVV ✚ G3 ☒ Stationsplein 10,
Leidseplein VVV ✚ D6 ☒ Leidseplein 1
Holland Tourism International (HTI)
✚ Off map ☒ Schiphol Airport

EMERGENCY PHONE NUMBERS

Police, ambulance, fire	☎ 112
Tourist Medical Service	☎ 5923355
Automobile Emergency (ANWB)	☎ 0800/0888
Lost credit cards	American Express ☎ 5048666, Diners Club ☎ 6545511, Master/Eurocard ☎ 030/2835555, Visa ☎ 6600611
Sexual Advice	☎ 0800/0224176
Crisis Helpline	☎ 6757575

EMBASSIES AND CONSULATES

American Consulate	☒ Museumplein 19 ☎ 5755309
British Consulate	☒ Koningslaan 44 ☎ 6764343
Australian Embassy	☒ Carnegielaan 4a, The Hague ☎ 070/3108200
Canadian Embassy	☒ Sophialaan 7, The Hague ☎ 070/3111600
New Zealand Embassy	☒ Carnegielaan 10, The Hague ☎ 070/3469324
Irish Embassy	☒ Dr Kuyperstraat 9, The Hague ☎ 070/3630993
South African Embassy	☒ Wassenaarseweg 40, The Hague ☎ 070/3924501

Language

BASICS

ja	yes
nee	no
alstublieft	please
bedankt	thank you
hallo	hello
goedemorgen	good morning
goedemiddag	good afternoon
goedenavond	good evening
welterusten	good night
dag	goodbye

USEFUL WORDS

goed/slecht	good/bad
groot/klein	big/small
warm/koud	hot/cold
nieuw/oud	new/old
open/gesloten	open/closed
ingang/uitgang	entrance/exit
heren/damen	men's/women's
wc	lavatory
vrij/bezet	free/occupied
ver/dichtbij	far/near
links/rechts	left/right
rechtdoor	straight ahead

NUMBERS

een	1
twee	2
drie	3
vier	4
vijf	5
zes	6
zeven	7
acht	8
negen	9
tien	10
elf	11
twaalf	12
dertien	13
veertien	14
vijftien	15
zestien	16
zeventien	17
achttien	18
negentien	19
twintig	20
dertig	30
veertig	40
vijftig	50
honderd	100
duizend	1,000

USEFUL PHRASES

Spreekt u engels?	Do you speak English?
Zijn er nog kamers vrij?	Do you have a vacant room?
met bad/douche	with bath/shower
Ik versta u niet	I don't understand
Waar is/zijn?	Where is/are ..?
Hoe ver is het naar?	How far is it to ..?
Hoeveel kost dit? ...	How much does this cost?
Hoe laat gaat u open?	What time do you open?
Hoe laat gaat u dicht?	What time do you close?
Kunt u mij helpen?	Can you help me?

DAYS AND TIMES

Zondag	Sunday
Maandag	Monday
Dinsdag	Tuesday
Woensdag	Wednesday
Donderdag	Thursday
Vrijdag	Friday
Zaterdag	Saturday
vandaag	today
gisteren	yesterday
morgen	tomorrow

Timeline

BEFORE 1400

Herring fishermen settle on the Amstel in the 13th century and a dam is built across the river. In 1300 the settlement is given city status and in 1345 becomes an important pilgrimage place and a major trading post although remaining very small.

HERRING CITY

If there had been no herring, Amsterdam might never have come into existence. In the Middle Ages, the Dutch discovered how to cure these fish, and they became a staple food. Herring fishermen built a dam across the Amstel river and a small fishing village developed, Amstelledamme. Its site is now the Dam, Amsterdam's main square.

1425 First horseshoe canal, the Singel, is dug.

1517 Protestant Reformation in Germany. In subsequent decades Lutheran and Calvinist ideas take root in the city.

1519 Amsterdam becomes part of the Spanish empire and nominally Catholic.

1567–68 Start of the Eighty Years' War against Spanish rule.

1578 Amsterdam capitulates to William of Orange. Calvinists take power.

17th century Dutch Golden Age. Amsterdam becomes the most important port in the world.

1602 United East India Company founded. It collapses in 1799.

1613 Work starts on the Gratchtengordel (Canal Ring).

1642 Rembrandt paints his classic work *The Night Watch*.

1648 End of war with Spain.

1652–54 First of a series of wars with Britain for maritime supremacy.

1806 Napoleon takes over the republic.

1813 Prince William returns from exile. Crowned William I in 1814.

1876 North Sea Canal opens, bringing new prosperity.

1928 Amsterdam hosts the Olympics.

1914–18 World War I. The Netherlands is neutral.

1940–45 German Occupation in World War II. Anne Frank goes into hiding.

1960s–70s Hippies flock to the city from Europe.

1964–67 Antiestablishment riots are rife in the city.

1980 Queen Beatrix crowned. The city is named Holland's capital.

1989 City government falls because of weak anti-vehicle laws. New laws eventually free the city of traffic.

1990 Van Gogh centenary exhibition attracts 890,000 visitors.

1998–99 Redevelopment of Museumplein.

2006 Rembrandt 400 celebrates the 400th anniversary of the birth of the artist.

A POPULAR MONARCH

Beatrix, Queen of the Netherlands, came to the throne when her mother Queen Juliana, abdicated on 30 April 1980. Beatrix, born in 1938, was crowned at the Nieuwe Kerk. Her great popularity is reflected on her official birthday (*Koninginnedag*, 30 April)—an exuberantly celebrated national holiday.

From far left: Napoleon Bonaparte; ornate ceramic panel with portrait of artist Frans Hals; waiting outside Anne Frank's house; statue of Rembrandt; Neptune on the Amsterdam

Index

CITYPACK TOP 25
Amsterdam

WRITTEN BY Teresa Fisher
ADDITIONAL WRITING Hilary Weston and Jackie Staddon
DESIGN CONCEPT AND DESIGN WORK Kate Harling
INDEXER Marie Lorimer
EDITORIAL MANAGEMENT Apostrophe S Limited
SERIES EDITOR Paul Mitchell

© **AUTOMOBILE ASSOCIATION DEVELOPMENTS LIMITED 2007**

First published 1997
Colour separation by Keenes
Printed and bound by Leo, China

A CIP catalogue record for this book is available from the British Library.

ISBN 978-0-7495-5082-0

Published by AA Publishing, a trading name of Automobile Association Developments Limited, whose registered office is Fanum House, Basing View, Basingstoke, Hampshire RG21 4EA. Registered number 1878835.

A02815
Maps in this title produced from mapping © MAIRDUMONT / Falk Verlag 2006
Transport map © Communicarta Ltd, UK

The Automobile Association wishes to thank the following photographers, companies and picture libraries for their assistance in the preparation of this book.

Abbreviations for the picture credits are as follows – (t) top; (b) bottom; (l) left; (r) right; (c) centre; (AA) AA World Travel Library; (IFC) Inside Front Cover.

Front cover image: AA/K Paterson
Back cover images: (a) AA/A Kouprianoff, (b) AA/C Sawyer, (c) AA/K Paterson, (d) AA/K Paterson

IFC i AA/K Paterson; **IFC ii** AA/K Paterson; **IFC iii** AAK Paterson; **IFC iv** AA/K Paterson; **IFC v** AA/A Kouprianoff; **IFC vi** AA/M Jourdan; **IFC vii** AA/K Paterson; **IFC viii** AA/K Paterson; **1** AA/M Jourdan; **2** AA/M Jourdan; **3** AA/Jourdan; **4t** AA/M Jourdan; **4c** AA/A Kouprianoff; **5t** AA/M Jourdan; **5c** AA/K Paterson; **6t** AA/M Jourdan; **6cl** AA/A Kouprianoff; **6cr** AA/A Kouprianoff; **6bl** AA/A Kouprianoff; **6br** AA/A Kouprianoff; **7t** AA/M Jourdan; **7cl** AA/A Kouprianoff; **7c** AA/K Paterson; **7cr** AA/A Kouprianoff; **7bl** AA/M Jourdan; **7bc** AA/M Jourdan; **7br** AA/M Jourdan; **8** AA/M Jourdan; **9** AA/M Jourdan; **10t** AA/M Jourdan; **10ct** AA/M Jourdan; **10c** AA/K Paterson; **10cb** AA/K Paterson; **10b** AA/M Jourdan; **11t** AA/M Jourdan; **11ct** AA/M Jourdan; **11c** AA/M Jourdan; **11cb** AA/M Jourdan; **11b** AA/M Jourdan; **12** AA/M Jourdan; **13t** AA/M Jourdan; **13ct** AA/W Voysey; **13c** AA/A Kouprianoff; **13cb** Digital Vision; **13b** AA/K Paterson; **14t** AA/M Jourdan; **14ct** AA/M Jourdan; **14c** AA/K Paterson; **14cb** AA/K Paterson; **14b** AA/M Jourdan; **15** AA/M Jourdan; **16t** AA/M Jourdan; **16ct** AA/K Paterson; **16cb** AA/K Paterson; **16b** AA/K Paterson; **17t** AA/M Jourdan; **17ct** AA/K Paterson; **17c** AA/A Kouprianoff; **17cb** AA/K Paterson; **17b** AA/M Jourdan; **18t** AA/M Jourdan; **18ct** AA/M Jourdan; **18c** AA/K Paterson; **18cb** AA/M Jourdan; **18b** AA/K Paterson; **19t** AA/A Kouprianoff; **19ct** AA/A Kouprianoff; **19c** AA/M Jourdan; **19cb** AA/K Paterson; **19b** AA/M Jourdan; **20/21** AA/K Paterson; **24** AA/K Paterson; **24/25** Anne Frank House (photographer Allard Bovenberg); **25** Anne Frank House (photographers Allard Bovenberg); **26l** AA/K Paterson; **26r** AA/K Paterson; **27l** AA/K Paterson; **27c** AA/M Jourdan; **27r** AA/K Paterson; **28** AA/A Kouprianoff; **29t** AA/M Jourdan; **29bl** AA/A Kouprianoff; **29br** Circus Elleboog (photographer Jean van Lingen); **30t** AA/M Jourdan; **30b** AA/M Jourdan; **31** AA/K Paterson; **32** AA/K Paterson; **33** AA/M Jourdan; **34** AA/K Paterson; **35** AA/A Kouprianoff; **36** AA/K Paterson; **37** AA/M Jourdan; **40l** AA/M Jourdan; **40/41** AA/K Paterson; **40r** AA/K Paterson; **41t** AA/K Paterson; **41bl** AA/K Paterson; **41br** AA/K Paterson; **42l** AA/K Paterson; **42r** AA/A Kouprianoff; **43l** AA/M Jourdan; **43r** AA/K Paterson; **44l** AA/A Kouprianoff; **44c** AA/K Paterson; **44r** AA/K Paterson; **45l** AA/K Paterson; **45r** AA/K Paterson; **46l** AA/K Paterson; **46r** AA/K Paterson; **47l** AA/K Paterson; **47r** AA/K Paterson; **48l** AA/M Jourdan; **48c** AA/K Paterson; **48r** AA/K Paterson; **49** AA/M Jourdan; **50l** AA/K Paterson; **50r** AA/K Paterson; **51t** AA/M Jourdan; **51b** AA/A Kouprianoff; **52t** AA/K Paterson; **52bl** AA/A Kouprianoff; **52br** AA/K Paterson; **53t** AA/M Jourdan; **53bl** AA/M Jourdan; **53br** AA/K Paterson; **54** AA/K Paterson; **55** AA/M Jourdan; **56** AA/M Jourdan; **57** AA/M Jourdan; **58** Brand X Pictures; **59** Photodisc; **60t** Brand X Pictures; **60c** AA/C Sawyer; **61** AA/A Kouprianoff; **62** Photodisc; **63** AA/C Sawyer; **64** AA/A Kouprianoff; **65** AA/K Paterson; **68l** Jewish Historical Museum (on loan from NIHS, Amsterdam); **68r** Jewish Historical Museum (Photo: Liselore Kamping); **69l** AA/K Paterson; **69r** AA/K Paterson; **70l** AA/K Paterson; **70c** AA/M Jourdan; **70r** AA/K Paterson; **71l** AA/M Jourdan; **71r** AA/M Jourdan; **72** AA/K Paterson; **72/73** AA/K Paterson; **74l** AA/W Voysey; **74r** AA/A Kouprianoff; **75t** AA/M Jourdan; **75bl** AA/K Paterson; **75br** AA/K Paterson; **76t** AA/M Jourdan; **76bl** AA/M Jourdan; **76br** AA/K Paterson; **77t** AA/M Jourdan; **77bl** AA/K Paterson; **77br** AA/K Paterson; **78** AA/A Kouprianoff; **79** AA/K Paterson; **80** AA/K Paterson; **81** AA/K Paterson; **84l** AA/A Kouprianoff; **84r** AA/K Paterson; **85l** AA/K Paterson; **85r** AA/K Paterson; **86/87** AA/M Jourdan; **87** AA/M Jourdan; **88** AA/A Kouprianoff; **88/89** AA/A Kouprianoff; **90t** AA/M Jourdan; **90bl** AA/K Paterson; **90br** AA/K Paterson; **91** AA/K Paterson; **92t** AA/K Paterson; **92c** Digital Vision; **93** Digital Vision; **94** Imagestate; **95** AA/M Jourdan; **98l** AA/M Jourdan; **98r** AA/A Kouprianoff; **99t** AA/M Jourdan; **99b** AA/A Kouprianoff; **100t** AA/M Jourdan; **100bl** AA/M Jourdan; **100br** AA/M Jourdan; **101t** AA/M Jourdan; **101bl** Verzetsmuseum; **101br** AA/A Kouprianoff; **102t** AA/M Jourdan; **102b** AA/K Paterson; **103** AA/M Jourdan; **104t** Photodisc; **104c** AA/T Souter; **105** Brand X Pictures; **106** AA/C Sawyer; **107** AA/A Kouprianoff; **108t** AA/C Sawyer; **108ct** AA/K Paterson; **108c** AA/C Sawyer; **108cb** AA/S McBride; **108b** AA/A Kouprianoff; **109** AA/C Sawyer; **110** AA/C Sawyer; **111** AA/C Sawyer; **112** AA/C Sawyer; **113** AA/K Paterson; **114** AA/K Paterson; **115** AA/K Paterson; **116** AA/K Paterson; **117** AA/K Paterson; **118** AA/K Paterson; **119** AA/K Paterson; **120t** AA/K Paterson; **120b** www.euro.ecb/int; **121t** AA/K Paterson; **121b** AA/W Voysey; **122** AA/K Paterson; **123** AA/K Paterson; **124t** AA/K Paterson; **124bl** AA; **124bc** AA/K Paterson; **124/125** AA/K Paterson; **125t** AA/K Paterson; **125bc** AA/A Kouprianoff; **125br** AA/K Paterson